Great
Conversations

By Peter Anthony Holder

*To my lifelong best friends,
Mario LeBlanc, David Edey &
Detlev Schmalhaus with whom
great conversations are always a
blessing. And to writer and friend
Michael Libling whose inspirational
conversations went a long way in
the creation of this book.*

Published in the USA by:
BearManor Media
P O Box 71426
Albany, Georgia 31708
www.bearmanormedia.com

Printed in the United States of America
ISBN   978-1-62933-180-5 (hardcover)

Book & cover design and layout by Darlene & Dan Swanson • www.van-garde.com

Table of Contents

Introduction

In the almost forty years that I've been conducting interviews, mostly for radio, I never thought of it as just a job, but rather, an opportunity to have a real connection, often with someone I greatly admired—because, I'm not just an interviewer; I'm also a fan.

I've been lucky enough to have job opportunities that allowed me to pursue celebrities without having the spectre of deadlines or "must-gets" hanging over my head. I went after people who wanted to talk, and the ones who didn't weren't a big deal. I wasn't concerned with stalking or being paparazzi-like. I welcomed the conversations because people were welcoming. Plus, early in my career I learned, what was for me, a very valuable lesson.

In August 1987, Christopher Reeve was in Montreal to attend the Montreal World Film Festival. (Earlier that year, he and Morgan Freeman appeared in *Street Smart* (1987) that was filmed there.) As a young entertainment reporter for a local radio station, I thought it would be a good idea to get in contact with the big screen's "Man of Steel," so I searched out the hotel he was at, found his room number, and knocked on his door.

When I told him who I was and why I was there, Reeve's temperament was that of almost every role we had come to know him in. He was courteous, polite, and warm, but he was also not happy. I had broken the sanctity of his space, had not gone through more appropriate channels, and came to his hotel room unannounced.

Reeve politely told me my actions were unacceptable. If I had gone through proper channels, he would have the option of saying "yes" or "no."

Even if I had asked him on the street or in the lobby (where I had spotted him earlier), he could have accepted to make arrangements at a suitable time or declined.

The reason why this encounter was such a valuable lesson to me was because, even though I had managed to anger someone who was considered to be one of Hollywood's "nice guys," his demeanour in rebuffing me was forceful yet extremely kind. It captured the humanity of the man. His actions have played back in my head for years to follow, guiding me in my interactions with others. I have had conversations with people who agreed to be interviewed, who were far less warm and friendly than a seemingly angry Christopher Reeve. While he may not have been officially recorded and part of my great conversations, it was still a memorable chat indeed; one that I won't forget.

One of my other long-standing working relationships was with another festival of world renown in Montreal, Just for Laughs. I have worked with the festival in several capacities for the better part of twenty-five years, which gave me the opportunity of working, partying, and chatting with some of the biggest names in comedy that came through town. I actually used to take my vacation from my regular radio gig to work at the festival, and I did double duty, recording interviews for later use when I got back on the air.

On different occasions, I asked two of *NBC*'s biggest comedy stars for interviews. One was David Schwimmer from *Friends*; the other, Jason Alexander from *Seinfeld*. In both cases, the response was a polite "no." In the latter case, I was with another journalist when I made the query. As we walked away, my colleague turned to me and said, "Boy, what an ass!"

That was a response that I've never understood. Jason Alexander was in Montreal to work, and while he was there, like so many others who come to town for the festival, he was hounded by the big guns at *Entertainment Tonight*, *Access Hollywood*, and *Extra*, plus all the print and radio journalists who flocked to the city for the festival each year. Saying "no" to me was not a big deal. I asked politely, he declined politely, and we went our separate ways. We spoke later in a casual setting without microphones, just sharing generalities, but an interview was not in the offing, and that was fine by me. Unlike some others in my business, I don't believe a famous face or voice owes me an interview. What they owe me as a fan is a good performance. What they owe me as a broadcaster is absolutely nothing.

What I want to share in this book is the humanity of the folks that I did get interviews with, because communication was a two way street. Striking up a civil conversation usually brought the best out of people in return. I've always treated interview guests as if they were dinner guests in my home. My job was to make them feel comfortable enough to talk openly, without asking pointed "gotcha" questions. In the end, that's what led to hundreds of great conversations.

Cloris Leachman. Photo courtesy of CharlesBush.com

Chapter 1

Cloris Leachman

In January 2005, I experienced the agony and the ecstasy of talking to multiple award-winning actress, Cloris Leachman, in an hour-long live radio interview via phone. The ecstasy was Leachman's personality. Although her Oscar-winning role as Best Supporting Actress in 1971 came for her dramatic turn in *The Last Picture Show*, the majority of the roles she was celebrated for were in comedy. Leachman, even without the benefit of a script, was a hysterically funny woman.

The agony was that I was suffering from a serious head cold and cough, so every time she made me laugh (and I laughed a lot), I had to turn off my microphone, because in addition to the laughter, I was also hacking up a lung in the process. It was painful, but I just couldn't stop.

At the time of our chat, Leachman was winning rave reviews for her role in the film *Spanglish* (2004), a movie where she was a last minute replacement for Anne Bancroft. It reunited her with her old boss on *The Mary Tyler Moore Show* (1970), director/writer Jim Brooks. There was much anticipation in her possibly snagging another Academy Award nomination, but it just wasn't meant to be. However it was a jumping off point to talking about her process in playing a role. She peppered her answers with great insight and chuckling at the same time. Leachman didn't just play a role, she inhabited it.

PETER: What do you bring to a role when you, as you say, inhabit it?

LEACHMAN: First, I like to be as absolutely authentic and real as possible, not representational or naturalistic; I want to be electrifyingly real. It's really a real person there. Because there are other ways of acting that are very effective. For instance, like Bette Davis and Joan Crawford, where part of it is just to stand and deliver, let's say. If you have a role like that, where it's a colourful, strong role, you deliver a line. That's an expression, you deliver a line. But this is the exact opposite of that. You're really looking for the other stuff around the line; the real life stuff that the lines just come out or through them. I've had some wonderful lines to say. You do want to stand and deliver them, but you don't want it to be on a performance level, you want it to be on an absolute reality level; the way you really do it with real passion and deep feelings.

Leachman had the same feelings about characterization regardless of the role she was playing, from drama to extremely broad comedy. I brought up her association with Mel Brooks and the characters she played, such as Frau Blücher *in Young Frankenstein* (1974) and Nurse Diesel in *High Anxiety* (1977).

LEACHMAN: You have to really invest yourself, really mean it. Not just on an above-the-neck strength and passion, but down in your gizzard.

They say acting, especially in comedy, is all about timing. Leachman got her timing from the world of music. Her first love was the piano, and she is a classically trained pianist.

LEACHMAN: That's very much part of acting. All the different voicings [sic] in music and how some lower notes come in, and the timings, rhythms, and cadences, all that stuff is part of acting.

Music also played a major role at home with her kids.

PETER: When watching the movie, *Spanglish* (2004), and seeing the relationship you have with your granddaughter in the film, I get the feeling that's what it must have been like in the Leachman household with your kids, because your character in the film was very artistic, as are you, but, I assume, with less alcohol, I'm hoping.

LEACHMAN: Well, in my house I had five children, four boys and a girl. The two-car garage quickly became a soundproof recording studio, so there was all that kind of music being recorded in there. Then, in the living room, I'd be playing classical piano. My second son was a really fantastic drummer, just wildly good. He'd put on Tina Turner in the living room, set up his congas, and play as loud as can be. It was so loud, her singing and his playing, and I had spent three weeks putting down the right fingering for "Rhapsody in Blue." There was an actors' strike at the time, so I knew I wouldn't be working for a while, so I just thought I'd learn that. So, I was really practicing and I would play as loud as I needed to and I still couldn't be heard over Tina Turner (laughter). Then you go down the hallway on the other side and my oldest son would be playing either the guitar or the flute and writing music. And then my little girl was in her room, she was practically a closet singer, and now she's a wonderful lyricist and composer; and my fourth son, who is a wonderful singer and writes and plays some. So, there was a lot of music in our house, but every person had a different kind of music. We could never be *The Partridge Family,* because everybody would have another idea of how we would be, I think (laughter).

PETER: With all the things that you've done, and it seems like everyone in your family is multifaceted and multitalented, what is your passion? What do you get the biggest kick from?

LEACHMAN: Oh I guess it's just around the table (laughter). When we have dinner or breakfast together, it's so hilarious! It's just the funniest! I've just been sick that people can't really see the fun. Oh my God, just brilliant humour! You just beg for mercy (laughter)!

Leachman was born and raised in the Iowa countryside just outside of Des Moines. She later went to Northwestern University in Illinois. While there, someone entered her in a beauty pageant.

LEACHMAN: Somebody who worked for an ad agency in Chicago would come up to Northwestern University if he needed someone to pose for an ad. I did a few of them. Apparently, they were having the Miss WGN Contest, and so he put my picture in the contest, and I didn't even know about it until I came home one night very late and found this telegram saying, "Congratulations you're one of twenty finalists in twelve contests around the city." And so, I was supposed to be there the next night.

The telegram also stated she had to bring her talent, along with an evening gown and a bathing suit. Leachman was reluctant to go. She ignored the telegram and went to bed. The next afternoon, the ad man promised to drive her down for the contest. Leachman was still reluctant, but the woman she was boarding with in Evanston, Illinois also encouraged her.

LEACHMAN: So, they both talked me into it, and I went down there just laughing all the way thinking it was hilarious. Anyway, I won this darn thing! I played the piano a little bit and danced a little bit and sang a little bit and said, "What else do you want me to do?" And they said, "Take your hair down." I hadn't even washed my hair! It was up in a pin, like in the movies where you take off your glasses and let your hair down. But it had curled itself and it just fell around my shoulders, and they said, "Congratulations, you're Miss WGN!" I just laughed so hard, I had to be careful they weren't getting their feelings hurt!

With the victory, Leachman was asked what she was going to do on Friday night if she won Miss Chicago. This was a complete revelation to her, as she had no idea this event would lead to anything. She took a piano lesson, bought a new bathing suit, and eventually won Miss Chicago, which then put her into the Miss America Pageant.

While she wasn't crowned Miss America, she was one of the finalist in the Atlantic City pageant, earning her a $1,000 scholarship. Her parents had travelled for the event. Besides winning the scholarship, her father gave her a prize, as well.

LEACHMAN: He gave me $60 to go to New York for three days from Atlantic City, and I stayed eight years!

That pageant was the beginning of her award-winning ways. In addition to her Oscar, Leachman, at the time of our chat, was the undisputed champ in winning Emmys. She had eight of them. In asking her about her collection, her laugh-filled, bitingly funny answer literally brought tears to my eyes.

PETER: How many Emmys do you have?

LEACHMAN: Well, I guess I have a record eight!

PETER: Wow!

LEACHMAN: And I tied, when I had six Emmys, five of them were for different roles. And I was tied with Sir Laurence Olivier for the same amount (laughter), but he was kind enough to die so that he wouldn't, you know, be winning all the time. How thoughtful enough, the poor dear man. And now I have eight! And Mary Tyler Moore, it was so funny; she said, "You have eight Emmys?" I said, "Yes." She said, "I thought you had seven?" I said, "No I have eight!" "You have eight Emmys!" I said, "Yes." She said, "Well, I thought I had the most?" I said, "I don't know, I have eight!" (Laughter.) It was a lovely moment for me, I must say. Very exciting!

It was at this moment during the conversation that we both got the giggles. For the next forty-five seconds or so, I couldn't ask a question and she couldn't formulate a response. We were both just laughing so hard.

The story of how she got the role of Phyllis from the producers of *The Mary Tyler Moore Show* is one of legend and it speaks to her funny personality.

LEACHMAN: I went in there and I said, "Who's the big cheese around here? Who can make decisions?" And they pointed to this man. I went over and I sat on his lap (laughter)! I remember doing that and it was Jim Brooks! I really do love that man. He is a genius!

The popularity of the character lead to a spinoff series of her own called *Phyllis*, which ran for two seasons.

PETER: What was it like to step away from the ensemble cast of *The Mary Tyler Moore Show* and step into the forefront in your own spinoff series as the title character in *Phyllis* (1975)?

LEACHMAN: Well, that's a very good question. It's very tricky. You can't take a character out of an ensemble like that and just expect it to be like cake because the person is identified by the other people around the person. That's who tells you what you are. How they react to you, in other words. And I think being a sort of pain in the neck that Phyllis was created to be and now playing the lead on my own series as Phyllis, it was tricky to make her likeable and lovable as the heroine and still have the irritating funny stuff that her personality on *The Mary Tyler Moore Show* had. Thank God, I'm not a writer, and I didn't have to worry my pretty little head about it.

Leachman had been married to director and screenwriter, George Englund, for a quarter of a century and had five children together. George's mother was actress Mabel Albertson, and his uncle was actor Jack Albertson of *Chico & The Man* (1974) fame, so there was a lot of Hollywood background in the family. In 1979, George and Cloris went their separate ways.

Ironically, three weeks before talking to Leachman, I spoke to her former husband on the air, because he had written a book entitled, *The Way It's Never Been Done Before: My Friendship With Marlon Brando*. I was hesitant to bring up her ex, but much to my surprise, near the last ten minutes of our chat, she just blurted out a question.

LEACHMAN: Are we going to have time to talk about George's book?

I reminded the listeners of the title of George's book and mentioned he was Cloris' ex.

LEACHMAN: Well I don't like to say that [he's my ex]. I like to say that he was my once-upon-a-time husband. That has more of a storybook quality than somebody you blot out when you're finished with them. I don't like to have been so wrong as to have an ex. I adore him. I'm still madly in love with him. I still fall in love with him every time I see him again. I really do. It's just an amazing chemistry. [She then gave a glowing review of his book.]

PETER: Do you ever have plans to retire? Please say no.

LEACHMAN: Oh God, you'll have to get a lead pipe! I just can't imagine such a thing! I have a wonderful life. I wish it for everybody who would like to have a wonderful life; to be doing wonderful stuff with wonderful, creative people.

I reminded her of some of my favourite roles she had in the Mel Brooks movies, and right on cue, she conjured up *High Anxiety*'s (1977) Nurse Diesel, complete with accent.

LEACHMAN: It was the "drapesh." Dr. Ashley felt that colour has a great deal to do with the well-being of the emotionally dishhh-tuuurbed.

Again, there was uncontrollable laughter on my part, but the true miracle of the night was that after talking to Cloris Leachman for an hour, my cold had broken. She was just the medicine I needed. I recommend to everyone with a serious cold to take a strong dose of Cloris Leachman. You only have to contact a doctor if your laughter continues for more than four hours.

Chapter 2

Ed Asner

There is one actor in American television history who has earned Emmy Awards for playing the same character in both a comedy and a drama. Ed Asner has seven statuettes, and five for his portrayal of Lou Grant. Three of those were earned playing the iconic character on *The Mary Tyler Moore Show*. The other two came after his character was spun off onto the eponymous *CBS* hit drama, *Lou Grant* (1977).

I had a conversation with Asner in May 1995 while he was promoting his short-lived *ABC* sitcom, *Thunder Alley* (1994), where he played a retired race car driver. While most of the characters he's known for were somewhat gruff, Asner was a gracious and engaging guest, who not only talked about his current show but reminisced on being part of one of the most lauded sitcoms in television history.

His career didn't start in comedy. He found the idea of being a comedic actor somewhat daunting.

ASNER: I avoided comedy when I first came to California. The way to be discovered in those days was to guest star on an hour drama show and become the next leading man, or whatever. I didn't really put my toe into the water of comedy until I went up to read for *Mary Tyler Moore*. I was afraid of it. Not that I couldn't do an initial spark of humour, but I didn't know how to maintain it. I was afraid of not being able to maintain it.

Before his turn as Mary's boss, Asner survived as a busy character actor, guest starring on a myriad of shows either as authority figures, such as police captains and lieutenants, or as a villain. However, his combined twelve years playing Lou Grant solidified his persona, not only with fans, but also casting directors.

ASNER: They will typecast you no matter what happens, and I realized I do the same thing in observing other actors that I come to expect certain types of work from and kind of rear back when I see them stepping out of that mould, but fortunately for me, my agent and I pursued contrasting roles as much as possible, trying to stretch whatever I represent as much as possible. That helped in gaining other casting beyond Lou Grant.

PETER: For a while, you had a nice little role as Markie Post's Dad on *Hearts Afire* (1992).

ASNER: That was enjoyable.

PETER: That was fun to watch. Was there not a possibility of you becoming a regular at the time?

ASNER: Well, I think they either ran out of material for me or they felt I was like a 600-pound gorilla perhaps and would be crowding the two wonderful stars of the show, Markie and John Ritter, making it difficult to write for them. So, they began to peter out in terms of writing for me, and since I was only on for about a year, and I had informed them that I would be leaving eventually to get my own series off the ground, they probably decided they had spun out what they wanted from my character, then began to soft peddle it.

Thunder Alley wasn't the first time Asner played the lead in a sitcom. Back in 1984, he co-starred with Eileen Brennan in the short lived *Off the Rack*, a series about the garment industry that was off the air after only seven episodes. I was curious to know if being the lead in a sitcom changed his acting dynamic as opposed to being a supporting character.

ASNER: It is different. I guess it creates a mindset in you wherein if you're not in heavy one week or a couple of weeks, you're more patient. When you are a second or third banana, you start wondering how long with this trend keep up?

Going back to his classic ensemble series, unless you have a crystal ball, you can never gauge how well a show will do when it's created. Asner got an inkling of the gem he was on when he saw that first script for *The Mary Tyler Moore Show.*

ASNER: It was one of the few times I have surmised correctly. When I got the script and read the character I said, "God is this gold! This is the best thing I've read since Hector was a pup!" It doesn't matter what happens to it. The joy of being able to do this character in this script would be enough to satisfy me. When I got it and when we were guaranteed thirteen on the air, most of the other actors were worried. "Will we be picked up?" I had a wonderful out clause for myself. I just said, "Who cares! This is the best stuff I've ever done in television!" It gave me a great deal of security.

It's hard to imagine other actors inhabiting the roles made famous by the cast of *The Mary Tyler Moore Show,* but Asner, like all the other supporting characters around Mary, had to audition. While he only auditioned for Lou Grant, his co-star, Gavin McLeod, also auditioned for the role of the News Director, but McLeod said he thought he was better suited to playing news writer Murray Slaughter. So, when Asner got the role, who did he pattern his character after?

ASNER: I used a lot of my brothers as Lou. They're wry, sardonic, twisted-look types. I kept digging into my ditty bag and envisioning my brothers a great deal of the time.

The Mary Tyler Moore Show picked up many awards in its premiere season, including Asner's first Emmy. He had a fond memory of going back to work after the summer hiatus with the win under his belt.

ASNER: The first night back on *The Mary Tyler Moore Show* in the second year, I was waiting in the wings, having won my first Emmy, with Gavin and Ted [Knight]. As they played the music to make our running entrance onto the stage, I looked at them and my heart was bursting and I said, Boy, I could die now!" They looked at me as if I was nuts and said, "You go ahead; we have yet to win ours!"

Television history was made when Asner's character went from a half hour situation comedy to the lead in an hour-long drama, but it wasn't an easy transition.

ASNER: It was not only an enormously difficult adjustment for me, it was for everybody involved. Everybody thought that. I asked the two producers, Alan Burns and James L. Brooks of *The Mary Tyler Moore Show*, to be my producers on *Lou Grant*. They were happy to do so, and it was their idea to extend it into an hour drama. Everybody at the MTM organization, none of them had really put out an hour drama show. When we debuted on the air, *CBS* was so nonplussed that they had us billed in TV Guide as *Lou Grant*, a comedy. I think the public was quite shocked, too, because I think when they tuned in on *Lou Grant* they expected to see just another continuation of *Mary Tyler Moore* with slightly different guys. It took awhile, a great long while, a year or two, for the public to adjust. Fortunately, CBS didn't have any instant replacement for us, and we won awards in the first year. That gave us time to grow and really find our niche.

You could hear the pride in his voice when he talked about his most famous character. Something else Asner is proud of is his role as a political activist. In addition to several hot-button issues and causes he's been very vocal about, he was also in the 1980s the President of the Screen Actors' Guild.

He played a prominent role in that union's strike against the industry, a decision that might have been the death knell for his hit TV series.

PETER: One thing that also gets your name in the news is the fact that you are involved, or have been involved, in several causes and organizations, and have been very outspoken in certain regards to some things you have said in the past. I'm just curious to know if that has ever gotten in your way, as far as your acting career is concerned, because sometimes you get people out there, either people in the audience, or maybe the movers and shakers in Hollywood, who just want actors to be actors and nothing else.

ASNER: That's quite true. My Presidency of the Screen Actors Guild, coupled at the same time being one of the founding members of Medical Aid For El Salvador, created a conflict which eventually lead to a good deal of controversy and I think achieved the cancellation of the *Lou Grant* show.

PETER: The cancellation of the show itself?

ASNER: Yeah.

PETER: At a time when *CBS* could have probably used a hit, it seems rather harsh to do something like that without realizing *Lou Grant* was bringing in a certain amount of money to *CBS*.

ASNER: Well, I feel the same way. We were still a prestigious show. It created demonstrations outside *CBS* and all of that. It was 1982, the height of Reagan power. I think it was primarily in the hands of William Paley [former CBS Chairman] to make the decision to cancel it.

I've witnessed first-hand how Asner's activism can lead to animosity from his opponents. Even though nothing controversial was said in our conversation, those who have political gripes with him, such as his stance against the death penalty, feel compelled all these years later, to send nasty emails my way just because I talked to an actor they don't agree with.

Wanting to end our chat on a high note, I had to ask Asner about what is considered one of the best episodes of a sitcom ever.

PETER: How does it feel to be, not only in a television show, considered one of the finest comedies ever to come down the pike, but also when people talk about the funniest episode of anything they've ever seen on television, they always come back to *The Mary Tyler Moore Show* episode of Chuckles The Clown.

ASNER: And that's a story in itself. A number of people associated with the show did not have confidence in it. The actors loved it, and so when we got to work on it, and as we approached Friday night and the performance, we had a fairly aged crew, and with so many death jokes, we never got many laughs when we were in rehearsal all week on stage. We began to get a little nervous. At our final run through, the producers said, "We're in trouble, because we are about five, six minutes short. We may have to come back after hiatus and shoot an added scene." We felt the script and the story were perfect the way they were. We hated that thought. I don't know who said it first, but we said we have to get out there and play the hell out of it, which we did in front of that audience. For the first time in my life, when I laughed, I really tried to create the most intensive, loudest laugh and more continuous laugh. I kept pumping up the show with energy and adrenaline of that type. And lo and behold, when we finished, the audience loved it. When we finished, we had stretched the show the requisite five or six minutes it needed.

PETER: It's a classic piece of comedy. I'm sure you must be very, very proud of that.

ASNER: I am.

Thanks to reruns, DVDs, and the Internet, you can find Ed Asner's performances readily available. Most actors seem reluctant to go back and look at their work, but when it comes to *The Mary Tyler Moore Show*, that's not a problem for Asner.

ASNER: I must say, I watch *Mary Tyler Moore* and I'm amazed. I tend to joke with people and say, "I like to watch *The Mary Tyler Moore Show* to improve my acting."

Stellar performances and a mantle full of awards is proof positive that, as an actor, Asner doesn't have anything he needs to improve upon.

Chapter 3

Gary Coleman

I've always had a soft spot for child stars, those boys and girls with wild imaginations and talent, who made a living in the world of make believe. Through the years, I've talked to many juvenile actors, who had varying degrees of fond memories of their youth in the spotlight. Some loved it and considered it the best years of their lives. Others to a lesser degree, but they moved on to other things in adulthood. A few, like many horror stories you might have read or heard over the years, were scarred by it.

Of the ones I have talked to, who had less than stellar childhood memories of the business, most seem resigned to the idea of their career as a different time. Whether it was through maturity or therapy, they've moved on, or, at the very least, just learned to compartmentalize their past and get on with life. That's not the feeling I got when I talked to Gary Coleman.

Coleman became a star at the age of ten, when his *NBC* sitcom, *Diff'rent Strokes*, premiered back in 1978. He played the role of Arnold, one of two Black brothers adopted by a wealthy White widower who was also raising a daughter of his own.

In November 2004, the thirty-six-year-old Coleman spent an hour chatting with me on the radio. He was intelligent, well-spoken, and engaging, but you couldn't help but notice the underlying bitterness in his voice, even when he was talking positively about aspects of his life. At times, it was a somewhat uncomfortable conversation.

Coleman was also politically active. The year before our chat, he was a candidate for California Governor. He came in eighth behind the eventual winner, another actor named Arnold Schwarzenegger. Since our conversation came just two weeks after the U.S. federal election, when George W. Bush won his second term as President, I thought I would start off by getting his thoughts on the outcome.

COLEMAN: I am chagrined, disappointed, and ashamed, and it makes me want to come to Canada. When was the last time you guys felt like your election was bought and paid for by one of your politicians? Do you guys have an electoral college where there's actually a small group of well-educated people who will pick your Prime Minister for you?

After an extremely short debate on the differences between America's constitutional republic and Canada's parliamentary system, we agreed the grass is always greener on the other side and, bottom line, the wonderful thing about democracy is the population always gets the government it deserves, regardless of how many citizens choose to exercise their voting right. His laughter at my response was my cue to change the topic. We focused on what he was currently doing.

Coleman had several irons in the fire. One of them was radio. He let me know that while I was doing my homework on him, he was doing his homework on me.

COLEMAN: Oddly enough, I was looking over your resume and I noticed you do some live comedy radio. One thing I've been doing since November of last year is something called All Comedy Radio. It's a rebroadcast of edited comedy material from comics, and we do our own original material, as well.

Coleman expressed his love for the radio gig, something he had followed up on with previous radio gigs in Arizona and Colorado.

PETER: What about television? I know not too long ago you were on *The Surreal Life* (2003).

COLEMAN: That's right.

PETER: First of all, I've got to ask why.

COLEMAN: Hey, you know what? I've been kicking my own ass everyday since I did that show. *Why* is the question! The only answer I could come up with was, gee, the money must have really been good! (Laughter).

PETER: Maybe you'll agree or disagree, but I assume, because of your diminutive stature and your career as a child actor, you're the one child actor that for some reason people won't allow to grow up. Would that be a fair assessment?

COLEMAN: That's pretty much a fair assessment across the board. That's why I'm so multi-facetted with this new venture I'm doing with some of your fellow Canadians. It's called AFT.BZ [Arts Financial Trust Limited]. And with the Internet, with UGO.com and with the video game called Postal, I am trying to break out in other areas of media to spread myself around a little bit and get the adult credibility and get the adult admiration I like. I enjoy getting compliments and admiration from the adults who have followed the fact that time keeps moving forward and have moved forward with me and do realize I am thirty-six years old. I do what I need to do to keep up with the audience that realizes that I am an adult.

Coleman's work with AFT.BZ was as a spokesperson, touting their business model for financing movies. To hear him describe the venture, it sounded like an early version of crowd sourcing to make films.

COLEMAN: For twenty-four months, you can let us hold $500 or $50 a month, and we'll put the money in a trust account. A trust account is the best interest-bearing account going, better than most banks.

He went on to say the money would be invested in movies, TV, and other media with the profits from successful projects shared with the film going investors.

COLEMAN: And after two years, if you don't like what Arts Financial Trust does for you, you'll get your principle back with the interest it earned, because we want the common man to share in the bounty that is Hollywood.

PETER: That sounds like something that would absolutely terrify the studios.

COLEMAN: You know what? Good! (Laughter.) You know what? There are a lot of dreamers out there in the world, and a lot of artists, and a lot of struggling actors, who would love to be able to have the opportunity to make a movie, and banks and studios get in the way. So, what Arts Financial Trust is doing is providing an alternative. So, yeah, please, let's scare them!

PETER: It sounds like your goal is to put the passion back in the work for those who enjoy the work, whatever medium it is.

COLEMAN: You are very astute sir, yes! We were trying to put the passion back in. With the advent of reality TV, and 400 cable channels, and a thousand satellite channels, the passion has kinda died. So, we want to give newcomers an opportunity to break in and show their wares and show their work, and we want to give the common man an opportunity to earn some of the billions of dollars Hollywood makes, so that he can say, "You know what? I bought a ticket to a movie I helped produce!" That'll build a groundswell of pride amongst common people who make $20,000 or $30,000 a year. The reason I'm a spokesperson is because I want to help people get out of the just at poverty or just above poverty line.

I couldn't help but notice that his desire to help people achieve their passion within the entertainment industry seemed directly opposed to his own lack of passion about his early success.

Going back to his hit sitcom, *Diff'rent Strokes* (1978), his bitterness started to show when I asked a simple question.

PETER: Were there any high points to being on the show?

COLEMAN: I don't think there ever was one for me, because it was always just a job for me. Even as a kid, I realized, hey, I'm doing a job, I'm working. So, I took it as seriously as I needed to in order to have fun. After that, once it was five o'clock or six o'clock or whenever the nine-hour day ended, I went home and got involved with my model trains or my video games or other things and didn't worry about it. I didn't care about the partying or the political act of Hollywood. That just wasn't my thing. I was never curious about it.

PETER: Did you at least enjoy it in the years you were doing it?

COLEMAN: Somewhat. I had my regrets and I had my druthers. They fuel me to seek positivity and other opportunities now.

PETER: What would you have changed if you had the opportunity to go back?

COLEMAN: If I had that opportunity to make the decisions I made, you probably wouldn't be talking to me right now. (Laughter.) I would be in Zion, Illinois, and you would not know me. I'm sure every actor has a moment in his life where he wonders, *What if?* I work toward change. My life is about change and multiple successes and that's what I focus on, because I'm not always going to be an actor. I'm not always going to be working on TV or working on radio, or working in front of the camera. So, I've got to continue being a chameleon and reinvent myself.

PETER: Well, how did you get into it in the first place? Weren't you something like four years old?

COLEMAN: Between four and six. It was an uninformed decision. We had no information; we had no idea what we were getting into. And had we known, if someone had shared some truths, with myself and my family, like I said, more than likely you wouldn't be talking to me.

PETER: It sounds like if you had the opportunity to do it all over again you wouldn't do it all over again.

COLEMAN: Knowing what I now know—it's that hindsight rule—is evil! Knowing what I now know, yeah, you would not be talking to me.

PETER: We've had some child stars on in the past. Some of them have, quite frankly, very bitter stories to tell, but some of them enjoyed the situation. So, what do you think makes the difference in the outcome of how people deal with being a child actor?

COLEMAN: You know, I don't have an answer for that, because my experience with the business is so different. Number one, I don't have a curiosity bone. I am not curious about things that could hurt me, harm me, are dangerous, or are immoral, or will break the law. I'm just not curious about those things. So, you would have to have someone be like me and someone NOT be like me and run the experiment and see what the outcome is. Now my outcome is you're still interested in me, a lot of my fans are still interested in me as an adult. The Wayans Brothers started a Little Gary Clothing Line because they loved me as a person. AFT.BZ loves me because I am articulate and intelligent and I believe in their product. I try to be truthful and honest and forthright and all of those things no one gets credit for. I try to be those. I've reinvented myself and continue to reinvent myself to those ends and I've been trying to do that for the last ten years.

When you talk to someone whose life experiences lead to regret and bitterness, you often get to the hypothetical "what-if" questions, but in the case of talking with Coleman, it did nothing to derail the runaway train of negativity.

PETER: If you had the opportunity to do in the business anything you wanted to do right now—write your own ticket—what would that be? What is it Gary Coleman wants to do that perhaps some people won't let him?

COLEMAN: You mean a wish list?

PETER: Yeah, a wish list.

COLEMAN: Oh, I would love to play different kinds of megalomaniacal bad guys, or I would love to do science fiction. You know, I wanted to do *Babylon Five* (1994). That was one of my favourite sci-fi shows.

PETER: Did you ever get in contact with the producers of *Babylon Five* and let them know?

COLEMAN: You see, this is where the politics comes in. Yes, but no! (Laughter.) That's the best way I can explain it to you. I can't tell you what the reasons are I'm not doing sci-fi or fantasy. I don't have an idea. I don't have an answer. Your guess and your fear (laughter) is as good as mine! I definitely have an eye on maybe producing, but it's not real high on my list. Actually, the number one thing on my list is to be semi-retired, because after a while, the people who populate the business, who are all puffed up and egotistical and are in charge, can really wear your soul down.

Coleman also had a very adversarial relationship with his parents. The bitterness stemmed from their handling of his Hollywood earnings.

COLEMAN: That was the traditional same old tired Hollywood story. It's all about greed! Unfortunately, adults will play at being nice and fair and honest and upright, but when there's a lot of money involved, they all want it. It doesn't matter what the emotional connections are. I prevailed as best I could. By the time I got around to collecting, they had already spent it.

Coleman ended up suing his parents and his former business advisor. After a four-year battle, he was awarded $1.2 million by the courts, but his relationship was irreversibly damaged.

PETER: So, you don't have a relationship with your parents?

COLEMAN: Oh no, not at all. I treat them like the pariahs that they are.

PETER: And you don't anticipate any chance of reconciliation?

COLEMAN: Oh no, not at all, because they still believe I'm crazy and I'm wrong and I never should have fought for my money. MY MONEY! I never should have fought for it. So, I don't have the patience or the time for that silliness, so I just move on with my life.

Moving on with his life, for a time, meant taking up a job as a security guard.

COLEMAN: Being a security guard is the only other thing I know how to do. I did it once before, I did it again, but I probably won't do it anymore, because I already have five spokesmen jobs, so I don't really have time to focus on being a security officer—and a security officer is just a fallback position."

Coleman's medical background was no secret. His lack of height, reaching only four-foot-eight-inches and his cherubic face were a direct result of an early autoimmune kidney disease and the attempts to combat it. He had two separate kidney transplant operations: one in 1973, the second in 1984, and he required daily dialysis. It seemed fair to ask him how his health was. Still, he was combative.

PETER: I think most people are aware of the fact that, when you were a child, you had some health issues. How's your health today?

COLEMAN: My health today is very much in my control and it is great. I don't have any issues with my health. I have never had any issues with my health. The only people who had issues with my health are the press! Because hey, all bad news is good news! But you know what folks, I'm going to be around for a long time and you're probably going to hear my voice on the radio for a long time. And you're probably going to see my face on the TV somewhere for a long time. So, you don't have to worry about my health.

Listening to Coleman for an hour gave me the impression he spent his life trying to get some amount of respect from those in his life and from the entertainment community, so I asked him the question point blank.

PETER: Do you find part of the problem is Hollywood isn't giving you the respect you feel you deserve?

COLEMAN: You know, I can't entirely blame Hollywood for not giving me the respect I deserve, because you have to command the respect. Being four-foot-eight, 95 pounds, an intelligent Black guy who isn't Denzel Washington, doesn't always command respect. And you know what, that's a hard, bitter, nasty, hairy pill to swallow. But over time, you get used to it. So, that's why I spread myself out through other media, and through other outlets, and through other products and services and goods. Because I as an individual, I have no business and no right waiting on someone to give me respect. I need to go and do what I have to do as an adult to earn the right to live on this planet and stay on this planet. And that means I gotta be employed, I gotta be a mover and shaker, and I gotta satisfy the masses of people who do respect me as an adult.

The Gary Coleman I talked to was nothing like the boy we watched for eight seasons on television. The adult Coleman was intelligent and polite, but he couldn't mask his displeasure at the career that kept him in the public eye yet offered up only painful memories. He couldn't admit he had challenges, both physically and professionally, that were stumbling blocks to any long-term happiness.

Perhaps in his negative banter there was an optimism many who knew and worked with him missed. In his own words on my show, he promised he would be around for a long time. We would see him on TV and hear him on the radio, so we shouldn't worry about his health. He was defiantly positive. Yet, six years later, he suffered an epidural hematoma—a traumatic brain injury—the result of a fall down a flight of stairs. That fall was probably brought on by a seizure, one of many he had in a life featuring a myriad of medical emergencies. At the age of forty-two, he was dead. His quest for respect and happiness was over.

Alison Arngrim. Photo courtesy of Gor Megaera

Chapter 4

Alison Arngrim

S hakespeare wrote in Hamlet, "O villain, villain, smiling, damned villain!" It seems those who act out evil on stage or screen are the happiest, most well-adjusted people. That's been my experience in talking to actors whose characters you wouldn't necessarily want as your best friend.

For seven seasons, Alison Arngrim, played Nellie Oleson, the little girl you loved to hate on NBC's *Little House on the Prairie* (1974). In reality, Arngrim is easily one of the nicest, funniest, and seemingly happiest people on the planet. I've had the pleasure to talk to her extensively on four different occasions, the first time in April 2001. Right off the bat, her laughter filled the airwaves as she shared stories about her life and career and the affect she has on fans. Playing such a brat on television for years definitely had its benefits for her personality.

ARNGRIM: People are terrified of me. It's the funniest thing (laughter). I guess I was more convincing than I thought. I'm scaring people to death twenty-five years later. It was an enormous psychological release, to go to work and be able to scream at people and let out every hostility you had. That's one of the reasons people would often say, "How come she's so relaxed, why is she so nice?" I had nothing left. I had gotten it out of my system.

Arngrim had been a child actor from about the age of five, so she had been around the block once or twice. By the time *Little House on the Prairie* came along, she was a seasoned veteran at eleven. Like so many young actresses back in 1974, she initially auditioned for the roles of both Laura and Mary Ingalls, but admits she wasn't quite the country girl type to land either part. They kept calling her back to audition for other parts. When she read for the role of Nellie, they hired her on the spot.

PETER: Did it ever concern you, psychologically, when you sat down and said, "Well gee, what do they see in me for this role?"

ARNGRIM: Well, yes, I'm still trying to figure out if the fact they hired me so instantly for the part of Nellie upon my reading was an enormous comple-ment or a really big insult. I still don't know yet if I should be insulted by that or not! (Laughter.)

Before going on any further with Arngrim, I wanted to bring up the topic of her mother, whom, at the time of our first conversation, had died only a month before. Norma Macmillan was a very talented woman in her own right. While she might not have been a household name, her voice was known to generations of children. The Canadian voice actress gave life to such characters as Gumby, Casper the Friendly Ghost, *Underdog*'s girlfriend Sweet Polly Purebread, and Daisy in *Daisy & Goliath,* just to mention a few.

ARNGRIM: The thing that always struck me as terribly funny is she was also Daisy's mother and sister and, of course, Gumby's mother and sister. They would only have two people to do the voices for the whole show, and she was all the high ones. And those who are old enough to remember *The First Family Album* (1962) the parody of the Kennedy family starring Vaughn Meader, my mother was the voice of little Carolyn and John-John.

PETER: Based on your mother's talent and your talent, there was probably no way you could have avoided the family business. I believe your brother's an actor . . . .

ARNGRIM: Exactly, my parents were both actors. They were in the theater at the Totem Theatre in Vancouver. And then, my brother is also an actor, Stefan Arngrim, whom you see on *The X-Files* [episodes "Terma" (1996) and "Tunguska" (1996)], and numerous science fiction shows, and of course he was on *Land of the Giants* in 1960. So, the entire family were all working when I was a little girl, so there was no getting around it. I said, "Where's my audition? When do I go to work?"

While many child actors faced hardships either from the business or their own parents, Arngrim never had to worry about such a fate awaiting her. With her entire family as actors, it was more of a natural extension of life for her. She also credits what she called the enormous advantage to have landed *Little House on the Prairie.*

ARNGRIM: Of all the shows to be a child actor on, to at least be on that show with Michael Landon and that cast, really did wonders for me and protected me from what some other child actors went through. And then also I had the huge advantage of being Nellie Oleson, so I didn't have the psychological burden of trying to be this perfect, never upset, never angry, perfect little child, who never has any problems on TV, and then trying to reconcile that to real life. I was this vicious, screaming monstrous brat, who could get out all of my tensions and hostilities at will and throw things and break things. So, pretty much anything I did in real life seemed pretty nice by comparison.

Arngrim had appeared in commercials and shorter shoots very early on, but when she was ten, she got her first real taste of understanding that acting was first and foremost a job. She worked on a film shot in remote parts of Florida called *Throw out the Anchor!* (1974). It starred Richard Egan and Dina Merrill.

ARNGRIM: It was great fun, I got to go to Disney World, we were running around in the jungle in Florida, and I got to have all these adventures. But I was on location. I was out of school, I had a tutor on the set, and we worked unbelievable hours. I had to do night shooting. I had to do things that were sort of technically dangerous. That's when it was clear that I had gone into this other realm of childhood, like "oh, this is very different." Of course, that's also when I realized how much I really liked it!"

PETER: One of the things they often say about acting, especially in films, is actors aren't paid to act, actors are paid to wait. What was that like for a ten-year-old's attention span?

ARNGRIM: Oh . . . that's so true! We used to make a lot of rugs on the set of *Little House*. A lot of crocheting, afghan rug hooking, and a lot of crossword puzzles got done. We didn't have GameBoys yet. We had Rubik's Cubes, puzzles, crocheting, and knitting. You get a lot done waiting. You can study your part and still have time to do all your crossword puzzles. That is difficult, especially when you have a set full of children, because what happens is your mind does wonder. We did have our school work to do; we had the three-hour school on the set, but every opportunity we had to sneak off and, well, basically, get into trouble and run riot, we took it. So, a lot of time on the set, after there was a lot of waiting and it was time for us to shoot, was spent corralling the children and getting us back to the set.

PETER: I guess the advantage you had, though, was that you were on a set with other children, as opposed to being on a television series, where you might be the only child.

ARNGRIM: Oh thank God! That's one of the things I've seen that is very difficult for a child when you're on the set where you're the only child. The focus is very heavy on them. If something goes wrong, it's sort of like, "Well, they're the child, it must be their fault." They're around other adults, so they're expected to behave as an adult. All of their relationships are with grownups. That can be very, very difficult. When you're on a show, where at least you have a large group of children, you have an environment where it is like your school friends. You're not the immediate focus of everything for the adults. They say, "Well, there's a lot of children." It's not like, "Oh, it's THE kid." You are one of many kids. There's more of a family environment because there's a bunch of children. If the adults are giving you a hard time you can create your own little miniature society amongst kids. And that's what we did on *Little House* and it was a major advantage. I mean, Melissa Gilbert is like a sister to me, and we were able to create our own relationships unit.

When questioned about whether being a successful child actor meant she might have grown up too fast, Arngrim confesses that could be the case. Although, since she was from a Hollywood family, she believes she would have grown up faster than most regardless, just by her environment alone. With acting comes grown up responsibilities.

ARNGRIM: You're working and on the upside you do need to grow up because you are making a living. You're paying taxes, you are holding down a job. You are put in a situation where you have to take on responsibilities and pressures some people do not take on until much later. Depending on what type of show you're on, and who you're hanging out with, you may be exposed to things people aren't exposed to at nine, ten, eleven, twelve. And when you turn eighteen, if your parents didn't steal all your money, you have a huge chunk of change at really the most vulnerable time of your life—that late teens-early twenties—when they say, "Hey, have a bunch of money, see yah!" You've seen what's happened to a lot of people. That's a very stressful experience to undergo."

Arngrim's upbringing not only allowed her to perfect her craft, she also became very media savvy at a young age. When she turned on the TV or went to the movies, she saw people on the screen she knew. It wasn't until she was seven before she realized not everybody was in television and this was a special and unique profession. She had also seen how her family dealt with the business away from acting, handling the press, and conducting interviews.

ARNGRIM: Some of the actors, who were grown people but had never been on a series before, were surprised by interview questions or shocked when the interview came out in a magazine and it wasn't what they said and had all sorts of trauma surrounding becoming a celebrity. I didn't. I wasn't the least bit surprised by anything that came out in a magazine, because my family had been in show business for years, and I had seen my brother interviewed, and I had seen how his articles had come out. So, even though I was only twelve, and the other people were much, much older, I was more jaded and relaxed and sort of matter of fact about things like being interviewed by *TV Guide."*

Arngrim still managed to have a healthy appreciation for others in the industry and was capable of being a fan. Like most kids, she had posters on her wall, went to concerts, and had crushes on entertainers. She also collected a lot of autographs.

ARNGRIM: I have an autograph collection. I have autograph books. I've even written fan letters to people.

Because of her most famous role, fan reaction for Arngrim was often decidedly different than adulation. She's had to deal with people getting upset with her in person and occasionally received very bad service at restaurants. Once during the run of the series, she even got blindsided by two other girls.

ARNGRIM: I got beat up only once. I made the fatal mistake of going out in costume. It was very early in the show. We learned quickly never ever to do this. I went to a fundraising event with Katherine MacGregor, who played Mrs. Oleson, and it was an absolute PR nightmare. Nobody wanted to come near us. Several small children saw Mrs. Oleson in costume and cried. I'm dressed as Nellie, and people wouldn't come near me except for two little girls who ran up and kicked me right from behind and knocked me flat on my face. And they ran away laughing leaving me lying there on the sidewalk.

Arngrim left *Little House on the Prairie* before the end of its run. When her seven-year contract was up, they wanted her to resign for another long term. Had she known the show was only going to be on for another two seasons, she might have agreed, but the idea of signing up for another five or seven years was too much for her. Nellie Oleson was married off to Percival Dalton, played by Steve Tracy, and the character was sent to New York. Arngrim shared some interesting back story about the relationship of the two characters.

ARNGRIM: One of the reasons that episode [*Come Let Us Reason Together*] was so interesting was Michael Landon wrote all of it. That was very much about his life. He even went on *The Tonight Show* and talked about it. He wrote the episode based on his parents. He said his father was a short Jewish man and his mother was tall and blond and Gentile, and his parents fought bitterly about religion. And he said he always wished his short Jewish father would have stood up to his mother. Now, of course, hearing this realizing that [me] at seventeen years old, Michael Landon decided I reminded him of his mother, was kind of alarming. That's why the episode was so incredibly detailed and had such emotional impact. It's in fact Michael Landon working out his childhood issues with Percival and Nellie."

Over the years, Arngrim appeared on our show for a variety of reasons. In June 2004, she discussed her advocacy work, fighting for the rights of children who were abused. She became a board member of an organization called Protect.org as they battle State and Federal legislatures to toughen laws protecting children from predators, especially from within their own families. Her association with the group also led to her sharing her own story of being abused by a family member as a child. The loss of close friend and TV husband Steve Tracy to AIDS inspired her to work both as a fundraiser and political activist in a battle against the deadly disease.

The last time we spoke was in 2010, when she was promoting her book, which had the same title as her stand-up comedy act, an act that slowly turned into a combination one-woman show/therapy session. It was called *Confessions of a Prairie Bitch: How I Survived Nellie Oleson and Learned to Love Being Hated.*

Arngrim really has survived. In one of our conversations, I brought up her personality traits.

PETER: Alison, it's always a pleasure and a joy to have you on the program. Having had the chance to talk to you on more than one occasion now, with all you've been through and being a child actor—and we've talked to many child actors—you're just one of the most well-adjusted people we've come across.

ARNGRIM: Shocking, isn't it? (Laughter.) As I recently told someone, I was abused and I'm an ex-child star. I'm really way behind on that tri-state killing spree! I should be much crazier than I am. I don't always think of myself as well-adjusted. I usually tell my friends, "No, I'm the craziest person you'll ever meet." And they say, "No, you're the sanest person we know." And I say, "Well, that's unfortunate."

I don't really want to argue with guests I have on the radio, but on this last point, I disagreed with her. Her friends were right. She was well-adjusted and sane, and people within her circle, and those she fights for, were pretty fortunate to have her in their corner. Alison Arngrim wasn't mean or evil. She was just very successful at playing someone who was on TV.

Dick Van Patten.

Chapter 5

Dick Van Patten

Many stories about the early days of entertainment, from stage to film to television, warn of the plight of child actors. While the gloss of show business is a strong aphrodisiac for many, reality often tells us there are dangers lurking beyond the stage or screen. Child stars can be exploited, or fall into bad habits or with bad crowds. It's refreshing to come across someone whose acting career went from toddler to adulthood and they enjoyed every minute of it.

Dick Van Patten is best remembered as the patriarch on the hit ABC TV series *Eight is Enough*, which ran for five seasons starting in 1977. Long before his success as a TV dad, he was a child model, Broadway actor, teen radio star, and a mainstay of television in its earliest days.

I had the pleasure of chatting with him on two occasions, years apart. The first one was in 1997, when he was promoting a book about child acting entitled, *Launching Your Child in Show Biz: A Complete Step-by-step Guide*. What I remember most was his enthusiasm and how he relished everything that happened to him during his life and career.

Van Patten got his start literally in a baby carriage. His mother took him as a toddler to a talent agency. Between the ages of three and six, he modelled, earning $5 an hour—a large salary for an adult, never mind a child—during The Depression. Modelling wasn't his favourite thing to do, Van Patten recalled.

VAN PATTEN: I can't say honestly I enjoyed it, because modelling was very boring. You had to stand in one position for twenty minutes, and I didn't like it."

As a seven-year-old, the youngest age children were legally allowed to perform on Broadway, his mother took him to casting directors, producers, and agents. He said that his break came playing Melvyn Douglas' young son in *Tapestry in Gray*, the first of many shows in a row that he appeared in on the boards while growing up.

I find it ironic when talented people chalk up their success to luck. Luck doesn't happen if you don't have the acting chops to back it up. Still, Van Patten thanks his lucky stars for many of his career milestones.

VAN PATTEN: When I was fifteen, I got into a TV series called *Mama*," (1949) [based on the 1944 play and 1947 film, *I Remember Mama*]. This was in 1949 to 1958. And so, I grew up. By the time it went off the air, I was an adult at twenty-four years old. So, I was lucky to make the transition. A lot of kids don't make the transition. They're very cute for awhile and then, when the cuteness wears off, they might be in a big hit series, and the series goes off, and they never work again."

According to Van Patten, the trick is to stay level-headed and grounded. For that, he thanks his parents.

VAN PATTEN: The parents should warn the children like my parents did. They said, "Look, you're having fun and everything, but it might all end tomorrow. You're only as popular as the show you're on, so just take it all with a grain of salt and just do a good job." And I think it's an exciting life, I've had a wonderful time. My sister was a child actress. Two of my three sons were kid actors. I worked with all those kids on *Eight is Enough* (1977). I grew up on a TV series as a child actor. So, I know what I'm talking about. It was a great, great life and I'm very grateful to my Mother for getting me into it.

There's a knee-jerk reaction in the showbiz community to recoil when the term "stage mother" is used, but for Van Patten, it's a term on endearment.

VAN PATTEN: They say "stage mother" like it's a dirty word. There is nothing wrong with stage mothers. There *is* something wrong with someone who forces their kid into doing something he doesn't want to do. But if a child wants to do it, it's not easy for the mother to go back and forth to all those auditions and everything. It's very tough. If a mother sacrifices like that to help her child become an actor, I think she deserves a lot of credit."

While there is glamour in acting, first and foremost it is a job, and like other trades, Van Patten believes it's an occupation that welcomes children and keeps them busy. He thinks kids should work, whether it's delivering papers or doing odd jobs after school, because it keeps them out of trouble and builds character.

Van Patten also believes some of the tabloid pitfalls trapping a few child stars are only magnified by Hollywood, not necessarily fuelled by it.

VAN PATTEN: There are a few show kids who got into trouble with drugs and everything. Todd Bridges and Dana Plato from *Diff'rent Strokes*, but that had nothing to do with being a kid actor. There are a lot of kids out there who are on drugs and have problems who are not child actors. So, I don't think it had anything to do with it."

To stress his point, he brought up one of the children who played his son on *Eight is Enough*. The drug problems of then thirteen-year-old Adam Rich, who played Nicholas, garnered plenty of press. Van Patten tried his best to help, but says a drug addict really has to want the help before they are open to receiving it. Rich turned his life around and grew up to be a director. In talking to Van Patten, who kept in touch through the years, Rich echoes most of what Van Patten has often preached.

VAN PATTEN: "You know Dick; I didn't get into drugs because I was a kid actor. When I was on the set, I was working and I would go to school for three hours a day and work the other five hours as an actor. I never had time to get in trouble. But when I would go on hiatus and went back to public school, that's when I got into drugs, when I was working on the show, there was no time for something like that. People seem to think I got into drugs because I was a kid actor. That had nothing to do with it!" I think the public should know that. Those kids had to work five hours a day shooting on the set of *Eight is Enough,* then go to school for three hours a day. But the education is very good. When they would go back to public school, the kids on *Eight is Enough* were so far advanced than the kids in public school because the education on the lot was sensational."

Van Patten was very quick to rattle off a series of names of child actors who successfully transitioned to working adults.

VAN PATTEN: Some kids are lucky and made the transition. Jodie Foster, Ronny Howard, Kurt Russell, Richard Thomas, Richard Crenna, these were all kid actors, who made the transition and are still acting today and are very successful. Ronnie Howard and Jodie Foster and Sidney Lumet were all kid actors and are three of the biggest directors in movies today!"

PETER: As you mentioned, many of those child actors gravitate to behind the camera.

VAN PATTEN: Yeah, and some get out of the business completely, not that they wanted to, but the business lets go of them and it's all over. But the thing is, while they're working, they can make a lot of money because of the Jackie Coogan Law. Jackie Coogan was a big child star. When he was eighteen, he met this big movie star, Betty Grable and he wanted to marry her. So, he went to the bank to get the money he had earned and it was all gone. The parents squandered the whole thing. He went to court, and they made a law called the Jackie Coogan Law. He never got any of the money, but he did marry Betty Grable. But because of the Jackie Coogan Law, at least the money has to be saved for the child, so if the child doesn't make the transition, at least he's got a bankroll, a nest egg, to go into some other kind of business, buy a franchise, or go to college.

Having done numerous Broadway shows in his youth, Van Patten spent a lot of time on the road. Stage shows didn't start in New York. They travelled to places such as New Haven, Philadelphia, Washington, and Boston, to work out the kinks of their productions. I was curious to know if being a busy actor, especially on the road, robbed him of his childhood. Van Patten was adamant that this was not the case.

VAN PATTEN: I would always go on the road for three or four weeks and it was always great fun. We used to travel on sleepers [trains] because there were no planes then. It was an exciting life. And then you'd come back into New York and you only worked at night. And I remembered when I'd get a job I would look for the script, hoping there were other kids in the play, because there was always more fun when you had other kids to play with backstage. But even if there weren't, even if I was the only kid, you always had an understudy, so there was always a companion. And believe me, I think I had more fun than all those other kids who weren't in show business. I worked with the most fascinating people in the world, travelled all over. It was a great education and a lot of fun, I tell you. No one had more fun than me growing up on the theater.

In a 2004 conversation with Van Patten, we focussed more on his days in live radio. Before people saw him on television in *Mama*, he was playing the same role on radio, plus a myriad of guest starring parts, often as the off-spring of current and future big stars Richard Widmark, Agnes Moorehead, and Arlene Francis.

One such show was *Theater Guild on the Air,* which featured re-enactments of movies on radio, using the film's original stars. Van Patten played many of the kid parts.

VAN PATTEN: Harry Truman was President then, and he loved the show. So, we went to The White House and did a performance of *Father of the Bride,* with Spencer Tracy, Joan Bennett, Elizabeth Taylor, and myself. A special command performance! It was really exciting!"

While congratulating Van Patten on his career, he interrupted me when I brought up a classic short lived TV show—a spoof of Robin Hood:

PETER: You've been on stage, television, and films. By the way, I'm still upset at the fact they cancelled *When Things Were Rotten* (1975).

VAN PATTEN: Oh, you have good taste!

PETER: That was a great show.

VAN PATTEN: Let me tell you something . . . that show was ahead of its time. The show went on the air. I thought it was going to run for five years. People were standing in line to pay to see Mel Brooks' movies. Here they were getting free Mel Brooks in their living room, and they cancelled the show! It was so funny, and Mel Brooks is still angry. He'll never do television again. He can't believe they cancelled that show. But I'm glad you remembered. Most people—when I say *When Things Were Rotten*—they don't know what I'm talking about. It only ran thirteen weeks, however that's how I got *Eight Is Enough.* When the show was cancelled, Freddie Silverman—the head of ABC—put me under an exclusive contract, and he put me in a pilot called *Eight Is Enough,* and, of course, it was a big, big hit.

What I was trying to ask him was what he was most proud of in his long career. I didn't think it was possible to wring more enthusiasm out of his voice, but he quickly went back to the pride of working with New York stage's royal couple, Alfred Lunt and Lynn Fontanne, in the play, *O Mistress Mine* (1946).

VAN PATTEN: When I was sixteen, I got a job with the Lunts. I had to audition against eighty other kids, and they narrowed it down to three. We had to come back in the afternoon, those three, to read for Miss Fontanne. In the morning, we read for Alfred Lunt. The other two kids were Roddy McDowell and Marlon Brando. It was down to the three of us, and I got the job! It was a great accomplishment! It was a very large part. I think it was the longest juvenile part ever written. My part was bigger than Lunt and Fontanne's!"

Upon hearing word that he would be working for The Lunts, a former stage student of theirs, Montgomery Clift, who had just moved to Hollywood, called up his friend, Van Patten. Clift and Van Patten had recently finished a Broadway play together.

VAN PATTEN: [Montgomery] called me up and said, "Dickie, I hear you just got the job with the Lunts. This is the greatest thing that could ever happen to you. Everything I learned, I learned from them. They're the best, the very, very best!" So, I would have to say, I've had a lot of exciting things happen, but I think that was one of the best accomplishments. It's the thing I'm most proud of to get. You had to be good to get it. I guess I came off good that day!

Van Patten worked with the Lunts for four years, two on Broadway and two on the road, in what was a meaty stage role for a youth. He not only successfully raised his family within the business; he even met his wife, whom he was married to for over sixty years, while he was still a child star.

PETER: You have a successful career, and you've had a successful marriage, and raised kids all within the Hollywood limelight. Some people tend to think that's somehow impossible.

VAN PATTEN: No. First of all, my wife was also a child performer. We went to professional children's school. When I was a kid, I had to be excused on matinee days and I had to be excused for auditions. So, I went to public school for a couple of years, but then after awhile they refused to excuse me anymore. So, I went to a school that still exists. It's called Professional Children's School, in New York. It's a school for child performers, and they excuse you if you have an audition or a matinee. Or, if you have to go on the road with a show, they send you the work by correspondence. I sat next to my wife in the seventh and eighth grade, because she and her brother were the world's youngest ballroom dance team.

As the patriarch in *Eight Is Enough*, Van Patten's career came full circle. Being the adult working with kids, no one knew better of what it takes to succeed, and he marvelled at the craft of current youngsters he considered colleagues and friends.

VAN PATTEN: I grew up on a series just like they were doing, so I have a real bond between us. I also had a lot of respect for them because kid actors always come through. When you see a kid actor, they didn't hand them the job. They had to audition about seventy, eighty kids to get those jobs, so the one that gets it has to be pretty darn good. And kids always seem to come through. They never forget their lines. The grownups will, but the kids never seem to make a mistake. My heart goes out to them. I think they're terrific."

Dick Van Patten was pretty terrific, too. Throughout his career, his acting gift and enthusiasm made him just a big talented kid at heart.

Chapter 6

Karl Malden

Academy Award-winning actor, Karl Malden, had a very long and illustrious career, spanning over sixty years. During that time, he conquered stage, screen, and television. In 2004, he was about to receive a lifetime achievement award, the Monte Cristo Award of the Eugene O'Neill Theater Centre. I thought this was as good an occasion as any to talk to a thespian who quit acting. I say quit, because it's the word he used as opposed to retire. What's the difference?

MALDEN: Well, after a while you figure out *I've been here long enough. How many faces does an actor have?* He can only show himself so many times. And since I'm ninety-two years old, I figured I had enough. So, I just quit!

It had been a couple of years since he left the business when we chatted. His last role was a guest starring stint on *NBC*'s political drama, *The West Wing* (1999), playing a priest, but he didn't miss being a journeyman actor.

Early in his stage career, every play he was in took him on the road. In films, he was constantly on location. During that time, his wife raised their two daughters, whom he really didn't get to know while they were growing up, because he was always away. He missed them terribly, but even so, quitting the business was initially an adjustment.

MALDEN: Now that I've been home these couple of years, I've realized what I've missed. I'm beginning to know my family. I'm beginning to know my grandchildren better than I've known my children. And it's really a different life and a beautiful life.

PETER: As you mentioned, you didn't get a lot of time with your girls when they were growing up, but you ended up co-authoring your biography [*When Do I Start?*] with one of your daughters, Carla.

MALDEN: Yes I did.

PETER: Was that an opportunity to get to know each other?

MALDEN: The first thing I did was write the book. I wrote it for about a month. She came over one day and said, "How's it going?" And I said, "Well, it's going pretty good. I'm happy." She went to go home and she says, "Can I read what you've written?" I gave it to her. She came back the next morning and said, "Can I come back here and do it with you?" I said, "How's that?" She said, "I'll bring my laptop computer and you tell me the stories." I said, "Sure, but why?" She said, "I think you tell a better story than you write." So, she sat and did it, and I think it worked out much better. And I'm so pleased, it is true! If you ever have the opportunity to work with one of your sons or daughters in a thing like that, do it! It's a great experience. We laughed and we cried an awful lot. And I'm telling you, we know each other, like we've never known each other before.

Malden was indeed a great conversationalist—the kind of radio guest whom you didn't have to ask many questions of. All you had to do was point him in a direction and let him go. There was a time when he spent three years as the President of The Academy of Motion Picture Arts & Sciences, the folks who annually hand out the Academy Awards. I was curious to know what the job entailed, and his answer was whimsically delightful.

MALDEN: I don't know what the duties are for the other Presidents, but I'll tell you what mine were. I became President, and somebody had a bright idea. We have a beautiful movie theater, but they said, "The seats are terrible, they've been in there for twenty years. We've gotta change them." So, the Board voted on changing the seats. Well, we changed the seats, and someone said, "Listen, while they're out let's change the carpet." And the fella says, "Fine, let's change the carpet, and the same time, we ought to have the curtains for the screen match the carpet." Good! Well, while everything is out and gutted, why don't we paint the house? So, it started that way, and before it was done, the whole place cost about $7 million to fix! Then, another thing: we have a library, and there was a fund for it, but nobody was doing anything about it. And I called the man who was in charged and asked, "What's happening?" And he said, "Well, nobody is asking me to do anything." "Well, I'm asking you to do something!" So, he says, "Well, you have to come with me." For three years, we raised $12 million, and I had to go with him. And that's something that embarrassed me, but I did it. And we have now a beautiful library in Los Angeles. And it's one of the top film libraries in the country. And I'm proud of it, so that was another $6 million. So, whenever I met the Board, I'd say, "I'll be the President who bankrupted The Academy of Motion Picture Arts & Sciences!" So, that was my reputation!

Like so many actors of his generation, it was customary to adopt a stage name. He was born Mladen George Sekulovich to a Bosnian Serb father and a Czech mother. Back in the day, Mladen George Sekulovich was not going to fly on a marquee, so he became Karl Malden. I pointed out to him that real film buffs enjoy a certain movie parlour game. Whether it's in classics such as *On the Waterfront* (1954), *Gypsy* (1962), *How the West Was Won* (1962), *Patton* (1970), or his Oscar-winning role in *A Streetcar Named Desire*, (1951), Malden always had a way of slipping in his given name.

MALDEN: I felt when I had to change the name. I felt a little touched about it, and I thought my father would say, "Well, what kind of thing is this?" So, I made it a point, the first time you'll hear it is in *On the Waterfront*. It was put in there by the director [Elia] Kazan. And then I felt, "Well, this is good, I'll put it in every picture I'm in." In *The Birdman of Alcatraz* (1962), I couldn't find anywhere to say it. So, I told the prop man, "Put a sign over one of the cells and put 'Sekulovich' up there." So, when I brought in a new man in charge, I started down the row, "Jim . . . Jackson . . . Sekulovich," and went right down the line. And when my Dad saw the film, he called me up immediately and said, "My son, I want you to know, a Sekulovich was never in prison!"

Malden also spent some time doing live radio dramas. One such show was *Our Gal Sunday* (1937-1959), where he played the heavy for about a year. He became fast friends with another actor, Richard Widmark, who, at the time, was starring in his own radio drama in the same building, *Front Page Farrell* (1941-1942). After their shows, the two sometimes went out for a drink, but it wasn't the alcoholic binge fest often depicted as part of Hollywood's early legends.

MALDEN: Between the shows and after the shows, we go out for a drink with the rest of the people. We'd go to the bar and sit at the bar, and I would order a ginger ale and he would order a glass of milk! And that was our association for years. And we still talk to each other an awful lot of time.

Many viewers got to know Malden each week as Detective Lt. Mike Stone on the hit *ABC* series, *The Streets of San Francisco* (1972), a show he starred in with an extremely young Michael Douglas.

PETER: Someone like yourself—and again, we mentioned your Academy Award—sometimes you hear stories about actors who "pooh-pooh" doing a television series because they've had a career on the big screen and on Broadway. Was it a difficult prospect for you to come to television, or were you quite prepared to do it?

MALDEN: Well, I never did television before I did *Streets* [The Streets of San Francisco], and I must admit I'm embarrassed to say, that I "pooh-poohed" it also. I stayed away from it. But when the time came, I said to the agents, 'I'll do it, but I'm going to do it the right way. I'm either going to star or I'm not going to do it.' And he finally got me this series, which I starred in with Michael. And it's one of the best things I ever did, because I made a lot of money off of that show. It ran five years, and I followed that with a thing that ran twenty-one years: that's American Express Travellers Cheques [commercials]. And I tell people even today, "Don't leave home without them!"

PETER: Was it really twenty-one years you did that!?

MALDEN: I did that for twenty-one years. And between those two, I can say I'm sitting here talking to you right now (laughter).

PETER: When you did *The Streets of San Francisco*, I heard a story, and maybe you can share it with us. You're doing a scene with Michael Douglas, and Michael is the young whippersnapper behind the wheel of the car, and he just takes off down the road.

MALDEN: Oh . . . that was the first year. That was scary. We don't laugh at that much (laughter) but it happened! We went down California Street in San Francisco, Nob Hill. And you know San Francisco is a lot of hills up and down, up and down. Steep hills! Michael drives a car very well; he's a good driver. He went down California, made a left turn in front of a hotel. After a half a block, there's a hill. He didn't realize how steep it was, and he was going about 65 miles per hour, and before you know it, we were airborne. There was no street under us! So, finally I looked at Michael and I said, "What the hell is this!" And he panicked, but thank God we landed safe. It tore out the whole bottom of the car, but everything ended up all right. That was one of the first episodes we did. From then on, we'd still go fast, but believe me, we made sure of where we were going (laughter).

PETER: Michael was a young kid, one of his first gigs as an actor. You are one of the contemporaries of his dad [Kirk Douglas]. Who was he more afraid of, the producer, the director or you after that?

MALDEN: No . . . (laughter) . . . that's a tough one to answer. I don't think he was afraid of anybody. I don't. With me, there was no mention of fear at all. We just had a wonderful time doing it, because it was hard work, and if we hadn't had a wonderful time, it would have been terrible. We worked well together!

Since Malden was the star of the show, he did have a say in casting co-stars. He had never met Michael Douglas before, so he was called into the office by one of the show's producers, who said, "I want you to meet a young man, who I think will be good for you." Malden came into the office, took one look at Douglas, and said, "He'll do."

MALDEN: The producer said, "You haven't even talked to him." I said, "I don't have to." I looked at Michael and I said, "Are you a Douglas?" He said, "Yes." So, the producer said, "How did you know?" I said, "Look at his chin! That's Kirk!" And he was Kirk Douglas' son, and I said, "That's good enough for me. Kirk and I started in summer stock together for a couple of years. We've been very close. You know, he's a big star, and he went his way, and I went mine, but we see each other quite often.

Michael Douglas is not the only newcomer Malden has worked with over the years. He did two Broadway plays and three movies with a very young Marlon Brando, an actor he calls a genius.

MALDEN: In the first play we did, we both had small parts. The scene he had was about six minutes long, and when he left, the play stopped. I mean, the audience wouldn't let him leave. They clapped, shouted, and stamped their feet. And I thought, *This is sensational.* Then, I worked with him again [on Broadway] in *A Streetcar Named Desire* (1947), and I wanted to see whether it could happen again. I realized he had something no other actor I worked with had. And I wished I had known what it was completely, because I would have stolen it and used it. It's something he does, other people try to do it; they cannot do it. Only he can do it. On film, he can look at you and stop, and look at you for a minute, a minute and a half, and it's still alive. The boys are doing it today. They look and they look, but it's dead screen. It's a dead screen and nothing's happening. He has something that I wish I could tell you . . . his eyes, what it is, I've looked, I've worked . . . it's an inner quality he has . . . I wish I could explain it.

While most people herald the genius of Marlon Brando, to hear Karl Malden tout his praises to a degree almost downplays his own talents. Before I said goodbye to the Hollywood legend—I so much as told him so—reminding him that in his last performance as a guest star on *The West Wing*, he, too, filled the screen with his talent, commanding every aspect of his scene with Martin Sheen. It was therefore fitting that his life was now coming full circle, and the night after we spoke, he was being given the Monte Cristo Award of the Eugene O'Neill Theater Centre.

In his career, Malden had starred in many an O'Neill play, plus he did several tributes to O'Neill after the playwright's death, so he was honoured.

MALDEN: After all these years, they're giving me an honorary award, and I appreciate it.

To add a cherry on top, the next night, he was announced on stage by Michael Douglas. So, it's fair to say, co-stars and fans alike, we all appreciated Karl Malden.

Chapter 7

Steve Allen

The late night talk show is a tradition on major U.S. television networks, but long before there was David Letterman, Jay Leno, Johnny Carson, or even Jack Paar, there was the late night groundbreaking, ground zero host, Steve Allen.

Allen is what you could call a modern day Renaissance man. In addition to being a naturally funny TV personality, actor, and the original host of *The Tonight Show*, he was a prolific composer, who wrote over 14,000 songs, including the extremely popular *This Could Be the Start of Something Big*. As an author, he wrote more than fifty books.

In December 1993, Steve was a guest on our radio show. At the time, he was promoting his forty-second book, *Make 'Em Laugh*. He also had plans for his next two books to be released within, as he said, the next couple of months. I asked him where he found the time to do all the things he managed to accomplish. His response was matter-of-fact.

ALLEN: Well, I find a fresh delivery of 24 hours available to me every day when I wake up. And I'm a compulsive talker and communicator. And since the invention of portable tape recording equipment, I've been using that for the last twenty years or so instead of the typewriter. I don't write any better, by any means, since the ideas come from the same source, but I get a lot more work done. I'm just lucky enough to be versatile and fortunate that the world seems to accept whatever I crank out.

Steve's versatility was evident at an early age as a preteen. In school, he was involved with the music department, wrote for the school newspaper, and did plays, all activities he just carried forward into adulthood.

Make 'Em Laugh is almost like a primer on the art of comedy. It was a follow up to a previous book, *How to Be Funny*. Steve's belief was, "Everyone on earth wants to be funnier than he or she is, and there's very little literature out there, if any, besides my own that actually revels the tricks of the trade."

PETER: Since this is a primer, I'm just curious to know, are people naturally funny, or is this something they can be taught?

ALLEN: Both, really. It's not an either or situation. There are those who are simply gifted and you can make an analogy with any of the other arts. You can start with a bunch of ten-year-old kids, let's say a thousand of them, and somehow arrange to have them all instructed by the same teacher using the same printed materials and the same brand of piano, and so forth. And at the end of that process fifteen years later, you might, if you're lucky, have one Oscar Peterson and maybe a couple of hundred who could make a living at it, and the rest might turn out to have wasted much of their money, although they still could have fun playing songs at Christmas parties. So, it's the same with comedy. There are actual tricks of the trade. As I say, I've now written these two books, plus four others on the subject of comedy. If I were gifted at motorcycle maintenance, I suppose I would have written a book about that!

Many have learned those tricks from Steve Allen. David Letterman on many occasions revealed he was a student of what Steve did, an acknowledgement Steve relished.

ALLEN: Yes, I think it was very nice of David to do that . . . well, it makes sense to do it because it is true. But when I was doing my second talk show in the early 1960s, David used to watch it every night when he was going to college in the Midwest, and he has since reported he thought he would like to get into television and do that kind of a show. And he was nice enough on his last show for *NBC* to mention my name three times as the source of many of his ideas. The ideas such as walking down the hall with a camera, or pointing the camera outside on the street, and all that sort of thing, doing crazy stunts outside on the sidewalk, he got all of that from our early shows."

While some of the funniest gags on Steve's programs were well thought out, he wasn't always clued in on what the gag might be, even if it involved attaching hundreds of tea bags to him and dunking him in warm water.

ALLEN: I rarely bothered to sit in on those planning sessions. As a matter of fact, it was better when I didn't. The fellas on the show discovered I am funnier when I'm not too sure what's going on. So, very often, I was the one person on the show who did not have any knowledge whatsoever as to what was going to happen or had the bare minimum of knowledge.

The only hint Steve ever got that something was going to be messy was when someone in production would warn him with the term "under dress," meaning that he needed to add some sort of protective gear under his outer layer to his clothing.

He had a keen eye for talent, as he was preparing for a show that would air on July 1, 1956. In addition to hosting *The Tonight Show* on weekdays, Steve was getting ready for a new series airing up against Ed Sullivan on Sunday nights. He had been watching a musical summer replacement show featuring bandleaders Tommy and Jimmy Dorsey, when he came upon a young singer.

ALLEN: So, I tuned in the middle of the show and there was this unusual kid. There was something remarkable, something unique about him. I didn't even hear his name that night, but I made a pencil note to book him.

It was four weeks later, on his second show of the series (July 1, 1956), that he brought the country's attention to Elvis Presley. Presley wore white tie and tails, and he sang "Hound Dog" to a basset hound in a top hat sitting on a Greek pedestal. It should be noted, this was two months before the future King of Rock n' Roll would appear on that much heralded edition of *The Ed Sullivan Show* (October 28, 1956).

PETER: Could you have envisioned when you started *The Tonight Show* so many years ago, what late night television would turn out to be?

ALLEN: No, not even the question had entered our minds. Did we see it as a big deal? No, never once! You begin to notice your picture is on magazine covers and you get a lot of mail. But somehow, to me anyway, it seemed like I was reading about some person who bore a remarkable resemblance to me. It wasn't entirely me. I was just concerned with what I would do that given night to put on a good show.

PETER: How do you think television has changed since you did *The Tonight Show*?

ALLEN: Outside of the extrapolation of the form, nothing much is done that's new. There are two types of talk shows, as you are aware. One is the *Tonight Show* type, and the other is the theme show. But they both grew out of the original *Tonight Show* program. On certain nights, rather than do comedy and music, we would have a serious theme. In one instance, it was the political blacklist, in another instance it was narcotics addiction. In the third instance, we were given two hours that particular night and we did a hard-hitting documentary about organized crime and the extent in which it had hit New York City. So, as you see today, there are two types of shows. There's the Johnny Carson type, you might say, or the Phil Donahue type, and they both were part of the original conception. So, if anybody's doing anything new in the way of a talk show, I guess I've missed him.

The addition of the Sunday night program meant more hours of entertainment to fill. That brought new comedic regulars to the forefront. Future stars, such as Don Knotts, Tom Poston, Louis Nye, Bill Dana, Pat Harrington, Jr., Dayton Allen, and Gabriel Dell. One by one, these great comedy minds were added.

ALLEN: In putting the new team together [for the Sunday night show], I went back and recalled people who'd done very well on *The Tonight Show,* and that's how I got Louie Nye and Don Knotts. And then later, we added Tom Poston, and every year we added one or two of the new fellas.

As someone who considered himself an authority on comedy, there was a lot Steve Allen liked on television and he wasn't shy about talking out against what he didn't like. While he was quick to praise shows like *The Dick Van Dyke Show* (1961), *The Honeymooners* (1955), and *The Lucy Show* (1962), as classics of their day, he was also just as quick to strike out at so-called classics he thought were dumb.

ALLEN: A greater mystery to me is why there is such widespread nostalgic interest in really rotten old sitcoms like *Gilligan's Island* (1964) and *The Beverly Hillbillies* (1962). I mean, those were really dumb, dumb shows. And yet, they, too, have millions of followers, some of whom may be furious with me at this moment for hearing me say that. But never the less they're not to be mentioned in the same breath with *The Honeymooners* and *The Lucy Show.* They were a much higher order of comic art.

Steve also had strong opinions on contemporary comedy programs. While he enjoyed the likes of *Cheers* (1982), *Seinfeld* (1989), and *Roseanne* (1988), there was no love lost for *Married with Children* (1987).

ALLEN: That's a vulgar, low class, truly disgusting program, and I would be very surprised if any of the producers listening to me right now would feel offended by that. They are deliberately being low class and vulgar, as, for example, Madonna is. If Madonna were trying to pass herself off as Mother Teresa, she would be terribly insulted with people calling her a "slut" and "prostitute" and so forth. But that's exactly what she's presenting herself as, so she cannot be insulted. She thrives on that kind of judgement.

PETER: What about the more adult themes? You mentioned one of the shows you like is *Seinfeld* and he has touched on some very adult themes.

ALLEN: Yes, that's true, and I'm aware some people find it highly offensive. I'm drawing a distinction between the general quality of the show and the themes. You can again make a constructive comparison with *Married with Children*. *Married with Children* deals with sometimes shocking subject matter, but in a gross . . . lewd . . . garbagy way.

PETER: Locker room type?

ALLEN: Yeah, that would be another adjective you can throw into the hat. It's just hopelessly crude and very low class. It's not art in any sense, whereas the *Seinfeld* show is done with great wit. The writers are really gifted at writing comedy scenes. The performers are absolutely brilliant in the enactment of their roles. So, even though, occasionally, they might do a show about a theme others would find shocking, at least it's done in high style and that's better than the *Married with Children* approach, certainly.

Even though he had spent a lifetime in comedy, I asked him if he considered himself a serious person. He said he thought he was both serious and silly. Many of his books were serious in nature, including a couple he wrote on The Bible.

ALLEN: Yes, I am a serious person, but when I'm not being serious, I have a marvellous time and laugh, I suppose probably more than most people you'd know.

As a composer, he wrote a myriad of tunes, many of them hits, and he even earned a Grammy for Best Original Jazz Composition in 1964 for "The Gravy Waltz." His silly side also brought out some very funny parody tunes, such as "The Girl with Emphysema," a takeoff on "The Girl from Ipanema," and a song that poked fun at a popular Western Canadian locale entitled "Let's Go to Lake Louise and Banff."

ALLEN: I remember when I was a kid of about twelve, I saw a travel poster in a window someplace and the caption was, "Lake Louise and Banff." And "Banff" always sounded to me like double-talk. I mean, "Lake I knew, "Louise" I knew, and I could visualize a place called "Lake Louise," but what "Banff" was? So, years later, I wrote a song called "Let's Go to Lake Louise and Banff." You can decide for yourself whatever "Banff" means.

Here's just part of the lyrics:

> "Let's go to Lake Louise and Banff
> By twos and threes let's Banff
> Last time we did it
> We really did it right
> I don't know about you
> But I could have Banffed all night."

Steve was very generous with his time on the show, and this wasn't the only appearance he made over the years. That's not where his generosity ended. It had always been my practice to mail each and every guest on the show a personal thank you note, along with a cassette tape (in later years a CD) of their appearance on the program. Sometimes, I received a note in return, but most of the time the letter went unanswered.

A month after I wrote to Steve, I not only got a letter back, (see illustration) but a package. He sent to me fifteen cassette tapes with a wide collection of music he composed. It was just the kind of think Steve Allen would do, and, yes, the collection included, "Let's Go to Lake Louise and Banff."

STEVE ALLEN
15201 BURBANK BOULEVARD
SUITE B
VAN NUYS, CALIFORNIA 91411
(818) 998-5830

Fourth
January
1 9 9 4

Mr. Peter Anthony Holder
CJAD
1411 Rue Du Fort
Montreal, QC H3H 2R1

Dear Peter,

I just returned to town after an extended absence to find your
kind letter of December 10th.

Needless to say I enjoyed appearing on your program.

By way of making my thanks for your kind comments more concrete,
I'm enclosing a collection of audio-cassettes on which you'll
hear some odds-and-ends that I've written over the years.

All good wishes to you and your family for the New Year.

Cordially,

Steve Allen

SA/cg

Enclosures: Beautiful Songs 1 - 9
             Jazz 1 - 4
             Sophie 1 & 2
             The Bachelor
             Alice In Wonderland
             Flop Sweat

Letter from Steve Allen (1994).

Chapter 8

Bob Denver

Teachers are highly educated and not usually characterized as laid back. It was really against type when political science major and former high school mathematics and history teacher, Bob Denver, made his claim to fame with two iconic television characters: Beatnik Maynard G. Krebs on *The Many Loves of Dobie Gillis* (1959) and the bumbling but lovable title character on *Gilligan's Island*.

In January 1994, Denver was promoting his book, *Gilligan, Maynard & Me*, a look back at his very successful career. I was interested in talking to him about the book on the radio for two reasons: one, I was a huge fan of the many roles he played in my television viewing youth; and two, I was double dipping and prepping for hosting duties of a stage show for later that summer.

Sherwood Schwartz, the creator of *Gilligan's Island* and *The Brady Bunch* (1969), was set to be honoured with two special evenings at Just For Laughs, with Bob Denver at his side for the *Gilligan's Island* night, and Barry Williams, aka Greg Brady, for *The Brady Bunch* night. I was slated to play the role of a hybrid between Oprah and James Lipton for both evenings, so the live radio show was a pre interview to the night where we would all be together, along with an audience of 400.

I often wondered at the start of a conversation with someone, who was so recognized for a character, about balancing my queries between the actual man and the roles he played. The second I introduced Bob Denver to our radio audience, the first thing out of his mouth on the air was, "I suppose I should start with . . . 'SKIPPER!' (laughter)."

Undoubtedly his most famous role was that of the Skipper's little buddy, Gilligan, on a show that ran for from 1964 to 1967, yielding 98 episodes. Thirty years later, new generations were still laughing along in syndication around the world at the exploits of the shipwrecked castaways.

I was curious to know if Denver ever anticipated the popularity of the character he created.

DENVER: No, I would have made a better deal, Peter (laugh). I would have made *some* kind of a deal. It's been on the air continually for thirty years. And it's been fun to watch the audience, because it's been the same every year. Pretty much the same, except in the mid-1980s, the older folks in their seventies and eighties started taking the autograph pictures home for themselves (laughter). "No, that's for me, it's not for my grandson! (laughter)".

Denver wasn't the first choice to play Gilligan. The producers originally wanted Jerry Van Dyke. Ironically, the role that would typecast Denver for years to come nearly slipped through his hands, because he had already been typecast for playing Maynard G. Krebs for four years on *The Many Loves of Dobie Gillis.*

During the meeting he had with series creator Sherwood Schwartz, they quickly won each other over, despite the somewhat wacky premise of the planned show.

DENVER: When Sherwood and I got done talking, I was on the floor laughing when he told me the premises of some and the guest stars and things. I said, "Are you sure the network is going to let you do this?" And he said, "Yeah, I have permission to shoot the pilot," and I said, "Well, fine, it would be great." So, we shook hands and that was the deal. Then, we shot the pilot of the island of Kauai, and I still couldn't believe it when I was in Hawaii for two weeks shooting a half-hour situation comedy that was so stupid and silly. I figured, *Well, if it didn't sell at least I got a nice, you know, two weeks.* I stayed an extra two weeks, so I had a month on the island. I figured that was really nice. If it didn't sell, fine. Then, of course, it sold, and became a hit.

Since he opened up the door of the show being, as he said "stupid and silly," I informed him of the conversation I had a few weeks earlier with comedian and original *Tonight Show* host, Steve Allen. Allen didn't have nice things to say about *Gilligan's Island* or *The Beverly Hillbillies,* but criticism of *Gilligan's Island* was nothing new to Denver.

DENVER: Yeah, it's interesting. The critics just killed our show. I think out of hundred reviews there were ninety-nine bad and one good one, but it didn't bother us, because we knew we were doing something really silly and something very, very broad, a lot of physical comedy. But the premise, I felt was just really hilarious. And then, I had a cast that was excellent. Each person was perfect as the character. What's happened is it picks up kids every year. I understand why a lot of the intellectuals or the elite don't really get behind it, because it's that kind of comedy that you can put down really easy."

Another person who wasn't a fan of the show was actually on it. Tina Louise, who played Ginger, was publicly dismissive of the sitcom.

DENVER: I guess Tina wasn't too happy with the show, because, in *TV Guide,* I guess in 1965, she said that if she wasn't on it she wouldn't have watched it.

There was also a little confusion on Tina Louise's part as to who would get top billing, which Denver admitted was kind of baffling to him.

DENVER: Yeah, they had told her that in New York. They had told her that she was the star of the show. My problem is if you get fourth billing, wouldn't that be a clue (laughter)?

Thirty years later, Louise was not happy again, this time over Denver's book.

DENVER: She got very upset, because I said I heard her having sex in the dressing room next to mine. I didn't think that was very bad. It kind of struck me funny at lunch hour. I pounded on the wall and nothing happened. I mean, I couldn't shut it down, the noise was so loud. She got very upset, but I think now she's kind of taking it with a sense of humour. I hope she is.

PETER: When you shot the pilot and you looked at the script for the first time, did you think it would sell?

DENVER: You know, I had no idea. It was just so much fun to do that kind of stuff. Plus, I met Alan Hale. Doing that kind of physical comedy with Alan was the most fun.

PETER: Didn't Natalie Schafer, who played Lovey Howell, only take the pilot because she wanted to go to Hawaii?

DENVER: That's right (laughter)! Her story was she was in Acapulco or Puerto Vallarta, one of those cities in Mexico, on a vacation, and, at the time, her Mother was ill in Los Angeles, and a telegram came to her table at dinner. She read it, burst into tears, and all her friends who went with her on the vacation said, "Oh Natalie, is it your Mother? Is something wrong?" And she said, "*No! The pilot sold* (laughter)! That was one of her favourite stories. They kind of almost convinced her it wouldn't sell; it was just a vacation for her. And after we started shooting, she really got into it. She was a great lady!

The premise for a show was so ridiculous. You couldn't imagine someone being lost on a three-hour cruise for so long, but there was a time when the actual U.S. Coast Guard tried to rescue them.

DENVER: There was an Admiral in the East here somewhere. He was a retired Admiral, in his seventies, and he got the coordinates. We gave them out one time, the longitude and latitude, which, if you looked it up, was in the middle of nowhere in the Pacific Ocean. He knew the chain of command, so he called Washington, and Washington called Hawaii, and pretty soon they had one of the cutters steaming up. One of the young sailors came up to the Captain and said, "Sir, I think it's a TV show." And he said, "What, son!" He says, "I think it's a TV show, sir." They checked it out again and found out, of course, that it was. They came on the set—the Commander did—with this huge stack of memorandums and everything else that came out of Washington. We almost really got rescued.

Because of the worldwide popularity of the show, its stars couldn't find a corner of the globe where they could hide. When I asked him if there is someplace the show wasn't seen, Denver recalled a trip one of his co-stars took.

DENVER: Dawn Wells was on a Samoan island that they had to take an outrigger to get to and paddle out to it. She went into the chief's hut, and the chief's wife went, "*Mary Ann* (laughter)! They had no electricity, no TV, and it turns out that the chief's wife had gone to another island to study nursing and seen the show there."

As globally successful as *Gilligan's Island* was, it was important to delve into the first hit character that started it all off for Denver.

PETER: Before Gilligan, you played Maynard G Krebs on *The Many Loves of Dobie Gillis*. How was it creating that character?

DENVER: That was fun! He was a beatnik when he first started out, the first and second year. And nobody knew what a beatnik was except that they really liked music. And I made him a real Jazz fan, Thelonious Monk, and Bill Evans, and all the big Jazz people who were popular at the time. And I was left alone pretty much to create the character, because no one knew exactly where I was going with it, so it was really a lot of fun. For my first series and my first acting professional job, it was just a great deal of fun.

PETER: During the span of the program, were you actually drafted?

DENVER: Yeah, I was drafted. I had done four episodes, and I got drafted into the army. I went down for the physical and I went 4-F because I had a broken neck back in the 1950s. So, I went back to the set to tell them. I was so excited. I could go and pick up and do the rest of the first year. They had signed Michael J. Pollard to take my place as my beatnik cousin. I walked on the set and they say, "What are you doing here?" I said, *"I'M 4-F! They don't want me! They don't want me!"* And they said, "Yeah, funny, funny, when are you going?" I said, "No, really!" And they just wouldn't believe me. And then, finally, after three or four hours standing there, Max Shulman came over and he said, "Are you serious, you didn't get drafted?" I said, "No." He said, "Just go home. We signed this man here, Michael, for thirty shows and this is the first one he's doing. Just go home, please! We'll call you." And then they put me in the next week and they paid Michael off. He did one episode and got paid for thirty. He had come from New York, and he said, "I had heard of coming to California to discover gold, but I didn't know it was true until now!" (Laughter.)

From the late 1950s into the beginning of the 1970s, Denver had an amazing run of success, going from *The Many Loves of Dobie Gillis*, to *Gilligan's Island*, and to *The Good Guys* (1968). Not many comedic actors during that time who could match his success.

PETER: One of the shows I was a big fan of was *The Good Guys*.

DENVER: *Oh, one of my fans! One of my few fans!*

PETER: Yeah, I watched that. It was on for two years with Herb Edelman and Joyce Van Patten. When you think about it, you had a pretty successful run there. You went from *The Many Loves of Dobie Gillis* to *Gilligan's Island* to *The Good Guys*. You had a decade, where you went from one show to another. A lot of actors can't say that.

DENVER: Yeah, I had about eleven years starting in 1959 to 1970, and then I decided that was it (laughter). I just said, "That's enough. I want to go back to stage work." So, I was on Broadway for about four months in Woody Allen's *Play It Again Sam* (1969). He left, I took over, and then I took it on the road for about almost six or seven years. Then, I just proceed to do everything that was available off Broadway. I came on the circuit, you know, and dinner theater was very hot in this country then. It was hilarious! People came to see plays and they didn't even know what they were. [In a hick accent] "Whaddya call that?" I said, "It's a play." "No kiddin', how long's it 'bin' around?" I said, "About 4,000 years." And they'd say "*No kiddin!*" But it was really fun for people who would never go to the theater. They figured they would have to get dressed up. The wife would drag them and tell them it was a big buffet and they could eat all they wanted to and just be quiet during the show. We did good comedies. We did all the Neil Simons, my wife and I, so we had a great time.

While the fans he met as he travelled the continent remembered him for the nebbish-like simple characters he played, they never confused this learned former teacher for his roles. Like a teacher, Bob Denver has had a long-lasting impact on them from their youth.

DENVER: It's thirty years, and people have been coming up to me, and they know it's just a character I made up. It's such a fantasy, the whole show is. So, it's kind of fun, and they've always been polite. In thirty years, I've had no one come up to me with any kind of rude remark or anything that's weird. They just grin, because I'm in their childhood. The show is stuck in their childhood, and it's a real good memory for them.

Yes, it is a good memory. Whether you're watching a rerun of *Gilligan's Island,* or talking one on one with Bob Denver, it's almost impossible not to smile.

Buddy Ebsen. Photo courtesy of Kiki Ebsen.

Chapter 9

Buddy Ebsen

If you grew up in the 1960s and 1970s, you were entertained by familiar faces on television who were a source of enjoyment and comfort. One of those faces was Buddy Ebsen. You may have watched him as Jed Clampett for nine years on the *CBS* hit sitcom, *The Beverly Hillbillies*. Or later, in his seven year run as the wily detective on *CBS'* crime drama, *Barnaby Jones* (1973). While Jed and Barnaby where very different characters, they both shared a down home folksiness that was part of the DNA of their portrayer.

I spoke with Buddy in March 1994. The down home personality of the eighty-five-year old was evident in his first words of our conversation. He bellowed, "Weeeeellll doggie!" his signature Jed Clampett line.

Ebsen was promoting his autobiography, *The Other Side of Oz*. The title relates to his original casting as the Tin Woodsman in *The Wizard of Oz*. He had the role for ten days, but Jack Haley took over after Ebsen suffered an allergic reaction. His loss of the part was a bit of a double whammy. Ebsen was originally tapped to play The Scarecrow, the role later embodied by Ray Bolger.

EBSEN: Because I was playing the Tin Woodsman, they powdered me with aluminium dust. It got into my lungs, and I got instant emphysema, and it was very serious, so I was replaced. I was tabbed for the role of Scarecrow. They shifted me to the Tin Woodsman, because a very natural Scarecrow dancer came on the lot. So, I was fine with the Tin Woodsman until the makeup. The tin suit was a problem, too, because they'd never made a tin suit before. I luckily survived the whole ordeal.

The shifting of roles followed by the testing of the tin suit and the paint basically turned Ebsen into the studio's guinea pig, trying to find what worked for the characters. In the end, Ebsen was out of a role, but that didn't mean he was completely out of the picture. Fans of the film remember the cast locked arm in arm skipping down the yellow brick road. The long shots may very well be Ebsen and not Haley who is off to see the Wizard. The soundtrack also has hints of Ebsen.

EBSEN: They discovered you couldn't recognize me in the suit at a certain distance, so I think, in order to save film, they just used some of the existing stuff. Definitely, they identified me on the soundtrack. When we sing, "we're off to see the Wizard, the wonderful Wizard of Oz!" that song, it's me."

Ebsen's road to stardom started in 1928, when he first went to New York. The talents of the song and dance man were tapped for the Broadway stage. Although he was the son of a dance teacher, being an entertainer was not his original goal. Growing up in Florida, Ebsen had his sights set on the health field, because he was a pre-med student.

EBSEN: I wanted to be a doctor, but ran out of money when the Florida boom collapsed. So, my father was a dancing teacher and, unlike the shoemaker's children, those children did not go barefoot; they learned a trade. So, I had a trade to fall back on and decided to go to New York and see how far I could get.

Ebsen's father taught mostly ballroom, ballet, and acrobatic dancing, but tap intrigued the young would-be hoofer.

EBSEN: He didn't really attempt to teach tap until I saw a group of tap dancers on a stage in Orlando, Florida. I went home and I said to my father, "I saw the kind of dancing I want to do." So, he pulled out a book called *Clog Dancing,* and together we worked out the steps, and that's how I got started."

Buddy wasn't alone in his quest. He danced with Vilma, his sister, on Broadway, and she also followed him into the movies.

PETER: Stage led to film roles. You actually did some dancing with your sister on screen, correct?

EBSEN: I did one with my sister, Vilma. That was *Broadway Melody 1936.* That was our first film. We did "Sing before Breakfast," which was a number that had some popularity.

PETER: That routine was done on a rooftop?

EBSEN: Simulated rooftop. It was a kind of a milestone, because it was the first of a lot of successful musicals that were done at MGM.

PETER: You also had a chance to dance with Shirley Temple in the movie *Captain January* (1936).

EBSEN: Yes I did! That was quite an experience. At the age of six, she had the aplomb, the poise, and the intelligence of a grownup. She was a true professional at the age of six. My definition of a professional is somebody who does their job without making your job tougher. She was one in a million.

PETER: That was certainly a difference in height!

EBSEN: Yes, we cured that by lifting her up on this big sort of hogshead tub and dancing around it with her, reducing the disparity of our height.

Stage and film roles eventually led to television, but in 1954, once again,

Ebsen was removed from a part he was tapped for—the title role in *Davy Crockett: King of the Wild Frontier.*

EBSEN: Originally, for about two minutes, I was supposed to be Davy, and then [Walt] Disney saw Fess Parker in a two-minute role in a picture called *Them* (1954) about giant ants. And he said, "That's Davy Crockett." So, it was quite painful for a few days, until they decided Davy had a friend and I was the friend, Georgie Russel.

Ebsen believed his ongoing second banana status on screen was all about the nose.

EBSEN: I didn't have a leading man's nose. You have to have a straight sort of heroic nose. I had a sidekick's nose.

A life of either being replaced or playing a sidekick ended when the role of Jed Clampett came his way in 1962. The lanky 6-foot 3-inch Ebsen was pleasantly surprised with his new leading status.

EBSEN: The writer, Paul Henning, had the theory that most successful series were built around a tall man, and I qualified. That was instrumental in the first moves toward getting the part.

You never know when you have a hit, but Ebsen believed there was no middle ground for *The Beverly Hillbillies.* It would either quickly fizzle or take off.

EBSEN: It was so far out, as far as anything that had ever been done before. We thought it would either be a big, big success or nothing at all. So, if it was nothing at all, we'd be back to the drawing boards and we wouldn't be wasting any time. Luckily, it turned out to be a blockbuster.

As I pointed out to Ebsen, official retirement age saw his career hit another high note.

PETER: At a time when a lot of people are taking it easy and slowing down, you sign up for a television show that runs for another seven years, *Barnaby Jones.*

EBSEN: Yes, it was only supposed to run for a half a season, but it fooled them.

PETER: It was only supposed to run a half a season!?

EBSEN: It was really concocted in a hurry to replace an hour that fell out on the *CBS* programming, so they figured it was only good for thirteen weeks, but the ratings were so good and unpredictable they were afraid to cancel it.

PETER: Had you known it was going to go on for seven years, would you have been willing to sign up?

EBSEN: Sure, sure, it was fun doing. I mean, I didn't have to put on much makeup, I was more or less myself, and it was very comfortable.

PETER: Most of the people had known you by this time as Jed Clampett, and before that a song and dance man, and also on *Davy Crockett.* This was quite a change. You had done musical comedy. You had done comedy. Weren't they worried about you being typecast as Jed Clampett? What would Jed Clampett be doing as a detective?

EBSEN: Well, as I said, Barnaby Jones was more naturally me. I had characterized more as Jed Clampett, so it was easy to make the transition.

PETER: Since you say most people think of you as Jed Clampett, do you find it's sometimes difficult, they meet you and they think you are Jed Clampett, the expect you to be Jed Clampett?

EBSEN: No, I just give them a big grin, and they forget all of that, and say, "Hiya, Buddy!"

Looking back at his career, Ebsen thought television was a medium created to highlight his talents.

EBSEN: It was almost like it was invented to sell Ebsen. I don't act and project on broad lands, and this [television] supplied a certain intimacy that seemed to communicate to a multitude of people.

Ebsen also found success in his leisure time as an avid sailor. Back in 1968, he entered his catamaran, *Polynesian Concept,* in the prestigious Honolulu Trans Pacific Yacht race and came away with one of his many yachting victories. His win helped to popularize the catamaran.

EBSEN: There was a superstition that catamarans would capsize at the dock. The fact that an actor sailed one to Honolulu and won the race, I think it established catamarans as viable vessels. They figured if an actor can do it, I can do it.

Ebsen claims he has sailing in his blood. His love for the water goes back to when he was just four years old.

EBSEN: As a boy on a small pond in Southern Illinois, I used to paddle around on an abandoned springboard. And then one day, I stood up and I had a towel in my hand. I felt the wind catch the towel and it wafted me across the water. That was my first taste of sailing and I liked it, because I have Norwegian ancestry, so it just spoke to the blood in me, and I've been a sailor ever since.

The hour of conversation on the air with Ebsen was a love fest for fans of his two popular television series, but I couldn't let him sail off into the sunset without bringing up an issue that played out on our airwaves on several occasions with previous guests, namely, the criticism that *The Beverly Hillbillies* was sophomoric and silly. It was first discussed with Steve Allen, who had no love for the show or *Gilligan's Island*. I had given Bob Denver the chance to defend his show, and now it was Ebsen's.

EBSEN: When it was first reviewed, there were nineteen critics who said it was "corny," and so I wrote letters thanking them for their reviews and asking them what corny means. And how many letters do you think I got back? Nobody could really identify the word. To me, corny means the emotions you feel when the big chips are down, like when a child is sick, or when you're in deep trouble. And *The [Beverly] Hillbillies* touched on an understanding of those moments plus a feeling and a talent for humour, which did not really destroy, but mentally it healed. It was a kindly show and a funny show. That is my identification of *The [Beverly] Hillbillies*.

It was his definition of his classic series that echoed my definition of having a conversation with the gentle giant. Buddy Ebsen was kind, he was funny, he was gracious, and he was all heart, the latter being an attribute that was lacking from a famous character he didn't get a chance to play.

Christopher Plummer. Photo courtesy of The Pitt Group.

Chapter 10

Christopher Plummer

C hristopher Plummer and I were both raised in Montreal, but that's
where the similarity of our lives ends. Plummer was a trained stage
actor, with a long and illustrious career on the boards and before the camera.
To talk to someone of his calibre was to be aware that I was in the presence
of a theatrical giant. Many of the characters he played were larger than life,
because he was larger than life.

I had the chance to speak to Plummer in June 1993. It was a telephone
conversation, because he was in Toronto preparing to do a one-man show
called *A Word or Two before You Go*, a benefit to raise funds during the 40th
anniversary of the Stratford Shakespeare Festival. Plummer had spent many
a performance on their stages through the 1950s and 1960s.

While I rarely got nervous talking to people of prominence, I must admit at
this early point in my career, there was a bit of apprehension in being on the
receiving end of the deep, rich voice that had bellowed through the roles of
kings and conquerors. I had also been previously told that, while he could
be quite charming, Plummer could be very tough. I got a sixth sense feeling
that a promotional conversation of any kind was a necessary obligation, as
opposed to something he relished with glee.

PETER: *A Word or Two before You Go* is a benefit for The Stratford Festival.

PLUMMER: It's a benefit for them and it's being done on the festival stage. They asked me last year if I would go up and play again, and I said I couldn't this year, but instead I would love to give them this one-man show to raise money for the theater. And they all very nicely said they'd love it, so here I am. It's a show I think is very suitable for Stratford. It's very entertaining. It's filled with great and less great literature. It's a kind of personal story of my own in which I play different characters along the way, and I use some of my favourite poems, and I talk some of my favourite prose. And it's all linked by, sort of, my own story growing up.

PETER: You actually wrote and arranged this yourself, did you not?

PLUMMER: Oh yes. Yes, I've done it three times before and it seems to work like a treat. And I change it all the time, because, of course, one gets new ideas. And wherever we do it, I put some local feeling into it, like a story of the place, and I'll certainly have quite a few stories about Stratford's stage. I take it right through youth to old age and back again, and all the poems and prose I've loved all my life and grew up with. So, I was amazed, when I was finally asked to do it many years ago, why someone else hadn't done it before. It turned out to be a very personal evening, and the audiences like that, because I think they get to know me.

PETER: What was the idea that initially brought this to the stage the first time?

PLUMMER: Well, someone in my local town, when I was living in Connecticut in the late 1970s, asked me to do something for the town. They said, "You haven't done a damn thing for us yet. You've been living here for five years. Why don't you do something like give a lecture at the library and raise some money for some charity?" And I said, "Well, a lecture seems awful dull to me. Let me think about it." And I thought, well why not? Why not just do some wonderful stuff that I love to do, read poetry, or learn the poetry and prose, and then write a little story to go along with it. And it became bigger and bigger and bigger until it became a show.

Plummer had conquered every entertainment medium through his lengthy career from radio to television to film to stage. He loved doing it all, because he believed that variety was the spice of life, but there was one medium he truly missed.

PLUMMER: I would hate to do just one thing out of those four because each feeds the other. The one I miss most, funny enough, is radio, because that's a medium I grew up in. I grew up in Montreal playing on both the French and English network. And then I went to Toronto and played on the stage series with Andrew Allan, when radio in Canada was absolutely superb. It was their artistic identity back in the late 1940s. I miss that whole era. I've always loved words, and radio seemed to be the perfect medium for words, because you could imagine what the people saying them looked like. I always thought it was such a powerful medium, and I miss the drama we used to listen to all the time on the air. It's a shame it's sort of gone. Maybe one day it will come back.

Feeling a little more comfortable chatting with this master thespian, I thought it would be a good time to tackle the commercial viability of the classics.

PETER: When people think of classically trained actors, your name comes to mind, yet you have a very commercial aspect to your career and you cross back and forth several times. There is no area one can pigeonhole you in.

PLUMMER: That's good!

PETER: Do you find that's a problem sometimes, when somebody says classical trained or Shakespearean trained actor, one can automatically think somewhat stuffy?

PLUMMER: No, well they know me by now. They know that's not true.

PETER: No, but I mean do you find that's a problem generally? For instance, Kenneth Branagh and Emma Thompson have just put out the movie, *Much Ado about Nothing* (1993).

PLUMMER: I saw it the other night.

PETER: It has brought Shakespeare to a whole new audience. Initially, when people were talking about this film in pre-production, there was a groan from some folks, but people are really enjoying it. Do you find what they're doing is basically bringing Shakespeare to everyone and making it more viable for the general population for which it was originally written in the first place?

PLUMMER: Yes, exactly! And what is doing them a favour is the fact it's beautifully done. I've even preferred it to his *Henry V*. It's an absolutely beautifully-done movie. It's young, it's attractive, it's sexy. It's everything Shakespeare is and wrote about. It's only the dyed in the wool people who are always afraid that Shakespeare is scholastic and heavy, and that's not true. From going to the movie to the theater again, one of the reasons I like to do this evening of mine is to re-enthuse people, particularly young people, into showing them how entertaining great words are. And the fact that language, great language is slowly and slowly becoming extinct with the terrible sort of introduction of computerized education and computer everything. We forget the great language that is our heritage and the great enrichment to one's life it does bring. And that's one of the purposes of this evening of mine. It's to remind them it's not only enriching but it's a hell of a lot of fun!

Impressive as Christopher Plummer's career was, many might be surprised this classically trained actor was also, to use his term, "a slight Trekkie." It explained his joy in playing General Chang in *Star Trek VI: The Undiscovered Country* (1991). Plummer loved the show from its earliest incarnation in the 1960s through its reboots and spinoffs, including the theatrical releases. Plus, he was a fan of director and writer Nicholas Meyer. Not only did he believe *Star Trek VI* was the best film in the series, but as he told it, "It was also great fun to reintroduce myself back to Bill (Shatner) again. We had good fun talking. I think our conversation had not stopped from when we left thirty-six years before. We just picked up where we left off." It was a chance for the two Montreal stage actors to reconnect about their youth on the boards.

Our conversation was much more cordial than I had initially feared it might be, so this seemed to be a good time to bring up a topic I was warned about. It was said Plummer really didn't like to talk about what is arguably his most famous role, playing Captain von Trapp in *The Sound of Music* (1965). In a more recent interview from 2011 with *The Hollywood Reporter*, Plummer referred to it as his hardest role, claiming the film was "so awful and sentimental and gooey. You had to work terribly hard to try and infuse some miniscule bit of humour into it." While he had been gracious and charming when we spoke, I detected a little frost on the phone when I brought up the beloved musical. I mentioned when I told colleagues earlier in the day that I would be speaking to him, everyone started to sing "Edelweiss." I asked Plummer if the song had followed him all through his career.

PLUMMER: Yes, of course it has. It's a bit of an albatross, but it's a nice albatross to have done because it's such a popular movie. And it still goes on being a popular movie. It's just sometimes a little bit tedious because you think of all the other things you've done . . . of quite meritorious stuff . . . some people only know you from *The Sound of Music*. But at least that has helped in many ways. It has helped sell tickets to the theatre, so I'm very grateful to that movie.

That was a hint to move on. When a conversation occasionally went south, it helped to steer it in a direction of pride for the guest. Often that's children.

Plummer's daughter, Amanda, is a Tony winner. Plummer and his first wife, Tony-winning actress Tammy Grimes, divorced when Amanda was a toddler, so he didn't spend much time in her life while she was growing up, since he went on to live in Europe for two decades. Watching her on the stage in her Tony-winning performance as the lead character in *Agnes of God* (1982) was the joy of a proud father.

PLUMMER: I must say, when I saw her in that play, she terrified me. I didn't have any recognition of her as being my daughter, or a family member. She was so good in it. She was so foreign to me. I was terribly impressed with her.

PETER: Was there more anticipation before you saw her on the stage, more nervousness because she was your child, than even when you went on stage yourself?

PLUMMER: Oh, of course! Oh God, yes! You know you can take care of yourself. I've been through too many disasters to know that! Yeah, I was terrified until she walked on and then I totally relaxed. Then, she terrified me in a different way (laughter).

Clearly the acorn didn't fall far from the tree, and the tree itself had branched out to a wide range of roles. Plummer loved the variety of his work. He was an actor who abhorred typecasting and didn't have a genre preference.

PLUMMER: When you do a comedy, you put some drama into it to break up the monotony. When you do drama, you try to be as funny as you can. I mean, I love all commercial and classics, contemporary and classics. You must do them all, otherwise you get terribly stereotyped.

Getting stereotyped had a way of dulling down the edges and sometimes becoming boring. Christopher Plummer was never boring, whether he was on stage, screen, or in conversation.

Theodore Bikel.

Chapter 11

Theodore Bikel

While Christopher Plummer found success in the role of Captain Von Trapp in the big screen version of *The Sound of Music*, the character was initially brought to life on the Broadway stage by Theodore Bikel in 1959. Rodgers and Hammerstein specifically wrote "Edelweiss" for his rich baritone.

Another stage performance Bikel was well-known for was Tevye from *Fiddler on the Roof* (2000 tour), a role he began playing back in 1969. I was lucky enough to catch one of those performances in June 1996, when Bikel brought Tevye and a touring company to Montreal. It was a performance in which Bikel truly became Tevye, a role that was like a second skin for the actor.

Zero Mostel originated the part on Broadway (1964), and Topol played him on screen (1971), but through the years, Bikel gave him the most life, taking him around the world, logging over 2,000 performances, more than any other actor. When given the opportunity to talk to him, I was curious to know why this role, which, at the time, he had played for almost three decades, was so important in his life. He said in more ways than one, it was a role meant for him.

BIKEL: I'm not only close to it as a performer, but I'm also close to the material. When I was a young kid, my father used to sit us down in the living room on Tuesday nights and read stories and plays. And Sholom Aleichem, on whose work this [*Fiddler on the Roof*] is based, was foremost amongst the works he read. So, I had this with my Mother's milk or Father's tea, if you will. Plus, Tevye is almost identical in outlook and attitude to my Grandfather.

Although *Fiddler on the Roof* is steeped in Jewish culture, Bikel felt that the story spoke to a much broader audience.

BIKEL: The ethnicity of it is just the background of it. It's set in 1905, and conflict is between Russians and Jews, but that's just the canvas on which it is painted. There is a hook you hang a story on and if the story has a universal appeal, it doesn't really matter what the hook is.

To emphasis his point, Bikel recalled a time when he took *Fiddler on the Roof* to Hawaii.

BIKEL: Half of the audience was not only not Jewish, they weren't Caucasian, and I would come out the stage door, and the play has a very moving ending, and I would see these Chinese and Japanese faces being clearly moved. And I would say to them, "What does this play mean to you . . . Jews, Russians, Pogroms, what does it mean to you?" And they would say, "Tradition, tradition. We know what it means when children don't want to follow the tradition of their fathers."

I decided to dig a little deeper on the tradition aspect with Bikel.

PETER: Tradition changes, as time goes on, unfortunately. In this day and age, there seems to be a lack of tradition. Do you think a play like *Fiddler on the Roof* speaks even louder than when it first went on the boards over thirty years ago?

BIKEL: I have no doubt that it does, because we lament the passing of tradition and the fudging of the edges of tradition. This play, in a very human way, it brings back the fact that you don't really need modernity in order to exist totally and fully. You need a mixture of modernity and tradition.

PETER: You get to travel around to do this play. How do audiences differ from place to place when you do *Fiddler on the Roof*, or are audiences just audiences everywhere?

BIKEL: Audiences are audiences. And I must tell you, I played this for example in El Paso, Texas. Seventy percent of the inhabitants of El Paso on the U.S. side are Hispanic. We sold out every seat in the play and there was such a rapport, and such warmth of reception, you wouldn't have known we were playing to Hispanics.

Bikel started performing as a teenager. He always sang and acted, which fed his urge to express himself artistically.

BIKEL: I tried for a short while to be an agricultural worker and I was hopelessly bored by it. To me, it was meaningless. I'm sure to an agricultural worker what I do would seem meaningless, but that's the way of the world. I would stand around in heaps of manure and sing songs about the beauty of the work that I wasn't doing.

Bikel's career also included film, television, and recorded music with over twenty albums to his name, but like many actors, the stage was his first passion.

BIKEL: I do prefer the stage, it's really the granddaddy of them all. On the stage, you're there, it's live, you feel it. There's a beginning, there's a middle, and there's an end. When something's funny, you hear it right away. When something's moving, you get that intake of breath, and the stillness from the audience, that's all there. You do films, you always draw on your experiences with live audiences. You know how to do that, especially if you do comedy on film. You're working for a laugh that may or may not come six months later, but you're working basically in a vacuum at the time you're doing it.

In film or television, an actor plays a scene and then moves on, but on stage, especially in a long run, there's a repetitive aspect I was curious about.

PETER: When you're doing a play, especially one you're doing for a long period of time, do you find there are new things you discover within the character? You've played Tevye for quite some time now. Is it still fresh to you? Is there something new you bring to the character each night when you go on stage?

BIKEL: The play is always fresh to me, because it's not the audience's fault I've said the words before or I've sung the songs before, but there are nuances, obviously, yes, but they are minutiae.

Despite his connection to two larger than life characters, Bikel had such variety in his career that made it difficult for producers and audience to pigeonhole or typecast him.

BIKEL: Thank goodness, they can't! I'm versatile, and to some people, that seems to be a curse, because it rattles them and confuses them, but it doesn't rattle or confuse me! I rather glory in the fact I'm capable of doing more than one thing, in fact, more than several, and acquit myself professionally of them. For one thing, I'm never stale!

Being a character actor meant never really becoming a household name. Many who saw him disappear in a character on screen marvelled at his acting skills, but rarely have "Theodore Bikel" on the tip of their tongues. This hadn't bothered him.

BIKEL: That's fine! There are two types of actors: one is a personality actor. You take a Clark Gable and you can call him Joe Schmo, or you can call him Rhett Butler, or you can call him anything you want to call him, but he always walks the same, he talks the same, and he looks the same. That's a personality actor. On the other hand, you take an Alec Guinness, and you pass him on the street and you wouldn't recognize him."

Eighteen years after our first conversation, I had a chance to talk to Bikel once again. It came only seven months before his death at the age of ninety-one. By our second chat in 2014, Bikel had managed to rack up more performances and add more hyphens to his already impressive career that spanned more than seventy-five years. By that time, the Oscar-nominated and Emmy-winning actor was the driving force behind the theatrical release of *Theodore Bikel: in the Shoes of Sholem Aleichem* (2014), and he was also touting his memoir, *Theo: An Autobiography*. I wanted to know what his original career goals might have been.

PETER: When you first started acting, did you have a vision or a goal of where your career would go? In other words, have you been surprised in the directions your career has taken you in the last seventy-five years?

BIKEL: Thankfully yes, I have been surprised. I just set out to be a good performer, a good singer, a good conversationalist, an intellectual, a well-read person. I later branched out into places . . . and of course I'm also a liberal. I come from a socialist home, and my involvement with labour unions and politics followed naturally from that. So, as a human being, I was involved in causes. As a performer, I branched out into all of the aspects of performing. I started with the theater, which is the most important medium there is, but then I did TV and movies, and each of them demanded a different attitude and different technique. And I'm glad to say I was able to master them to a degree of professionalism and proficiency that proved to be right.

Throughout his career, Bikel has also taken up causes and been politically active. He was even at one time the President of Actors' Equity in the late 1970s-1980s, championing human rights causes. Since 1988, he had been the President of Associated Actors and Artistes of America. Sometimes, leading the political battle and taking up the mantle for social justice had a negative effect on other's acting careers, but Bikel didn't give that a thought.

BIKEL: No, I was never concerned. You know, you follow your beliefs wherever they lead you and consequences be damned! You cannot play games with your own intellectual honesty, and you can't withdraw. For instance, if you see injustices and you fight them and you tread on some toes fighting those injustices, yeah, your career may suffer, but I would not be true to myself if I would resist from entering the fight.

Talking about *Theodore Bikel: in the Shoes of Sholem Aleichem* brought us back full circle to the conversation we had eighteen years earlier and the books his father used to read to him from in Yiddish. It also revealed his experiences of living under the tyranny of the Nazi regime.

BIKEL: My life and the life of Sholem Aleichem intersect on so many levels. We had thirty-six loggings of his collected works on our bookshelves. Then, the Nazis came, and in short order, we became refugees, and they confiscated everything we owned, including the books. We had to leave with one suitcase each. What hurt us most was we had to leave the books behind. And my Grandmother actually liberated the books from the clutches of the Nazis, by sitting in the anteroom of the warehouse where they were being kept—a warehouse marked "Properties of the Enemy of the Third Reich." And she wept, she cried, until the guard in charge of the place said to one of his minions, "Get that old Jewish woman out of my sight. I don't want to see her and I'll sign off on anything she wants! Just get her out of here!" And he did, and she liberated our things.

Those valuable books were shipped off to Israel, where Bikel's family eventually settled. The package arrived in Tel Aviv with swastikas plastered all over the container, but they, like the family, survived.

When his father passed away, Bikel sent the books to the Yiddish Book Center in Amherst, Massachusetts, a place where they could be cared for and well protected, but years later he needed them again.

BIKEL: When I started working on my play and my film about Sholem Aleichem, I needed them, and I called Amherst, and they sent me the same set of books. So, books have legs!

Escaping from the Nazis was the focus of one of his greatest accomplishments on the Broadway stage, but while he was Tony-nominated for playing Captain von Trapp, the role eluded him when *The Sound of Music* made the leap to the silver screen.

PETER: I've had the opportunity to talk to other actors, who were passed over for film roles of characters they created on stage. I'm curious about how you felt for not getting to play the Captain in the movie.

BIKEL: Well, you know, for five minutes, I was upset about that, naturally, but frankly, it wasn't in the cards, because on stage the star of the play was Mary Martin, and she was exactly ten years older than I, which, on the stage, you could get away with. There was no way she could play this role in the movie, and since they couldn't take her, they couldn't take me.

With an illustrious career that spanned three quarters of a century, it seemed hard to believe that there was someone who couldn't take Theodore Bikel. He was an amazingly talented character actor, who, like the role of Tevye, was all about tradition.

Chapter 12

George Takei

Actor George Takei lived up to the adage of the *Star Trek* television series to "Boldly go where no man has gone before." The veteran of space via *Star Trek* (1966) saw his character, Mr. Sulu, go from Lieutenant to Captain within Starfleet on both the big and small screens.

Takei, born to Japanese American parents in Los Angeles, went from living in Japanese internment camps in Arkansas and Los Angeles during World War II to becoming an actor, director, author, activist, and an active member within the Lesbian, Gay, Bisexual, Transsexual (LGBT) community.

I had the pleasure to talk to Takei on two occasions, the first in November 1994. He was promoting his book, *The Autobiography of George Takei: Star Trek's Mr. Sulu*. Takei had put off writing about himself, but the urging of close friends changed his mind.

TAKEI: I had been planning on writing my autobiography for quite some time, and it took two of my good friends, one being my agent. The two of them ganged up on me and said, "Now's the time to write it." I had been demurring, saying I'm much too young to be writing my autobiography. You have to have grey hair and a lot of wisdom, but when the two friends, whose opinions I respect, told me I should, I finally decided, I'm not as young as I thought I was.

His autobiography was the first time many had found out about his early life as a prisoner of war in his own country. Spending his boyhood in intern-ment camps was one of the motivations for writing the book.

TAKEI: When I travel through the East Coast or the Midwest of the United States, so many people tell me they never knew something like that had happened in America, and incidentally also in Canada. American citizens, who happened to be of Japanese ancestry, were placed in those barbed wire enclosed internment camps simply because Americans couldn't draw that dis-tinction between citizens and the enemy with which we were at war. Suddenly, our citizenship evaporated, due process was thrown out the window, and with no trial, no charges, we were summarily rounded up at gunpoint. It seemed to me important for a country—for a nation—to certainly know about its glori-ous achievements, but also to know where its ideals failed, in order to keep that from happening again. I particularly wanted to write about that part of my life.

It was perhaps that experience and the teachings of his father that Takei became an activist later in life. America's wartime missteps taught him the ideals of a country were only as good as the people who gave it flesh and blood. Takei's father inculcated all three of his children with the importance of participating in the process.

TAKEI: This is supposed to be a participatory democracy, and if we're not in there participating, then the people that will manipulate and exploit the sys-tem will step in there. So, I've been a political activist all my life, and I think, in a large measure, it's because of the internment we experienced fifty years ago.

PETER: How does that come out in your acting? I know that, as an actor and a young man, especially being of Asian descent, there is this stereotyp-ing most ethnics go through in Hollywood, at least in that period. Was it a problem for you too?

TAKEI: Well, it's true, a lot of roles then were pretty stereotyped and pretty unattractive stereotypes, but I'd been rather lucky in my career. My first TV show was *Playhouse 90*, ["Made in Japan" (1959)], one of the most distinguished live dramatic television shows of that time. And my first feature film, which I got while I was still a student at UCLA . . . I was seen in a student production by a casting director from Warner Bros. and plunked into this movie starring Richard Burton [*Ice Palace*, 1960], who was an idol of mine, this legend of the theater and a skyrocketing young movie star. So, I've been enormously lucky, and the capper on the string of luck was meeting Gene Roddenberry and to be cast in the role of Sulu, which was a breakthrough role for an Asian American actor.

PETER: How did you get the role of Mr. Sulu?

TAKEI: My agent called and said he had an interview for me with this man casting a pilot for a science fiction thing and there's this role for a running part. So, I went and I met the man. As a matter of fact, when I met Gene Roddenberry, I mispronounced his name. I called him Mr. "Rosenberry," and he mispronounced my name—he called me "Tah-ky" [rhymes with "buy"], which is not an uncommon mispronunciation. It's pronounced "Tah-kay" as you pronounced it. So, we got started by mispronouncing each others' name. When he described the role to me, I knew this was a role I had to have and I knew there would be a lot of competition for it. So, I was really nervous about it. After a stressful, tense week, the phone rang again and my agent told me I had the part, and the rest, as they say, is history.

I asked the actor, who was well-known for his mellifluous voice, if he always wanted to be a performer.

TAKEI: Well, my Mother says I made my theatrical debut in the maternity ward. She says when she heard my centurion yowl, she knew she had a ham on her hands. As far back as I can remember, I was putting on plays in the backyard and grammar school skits, junior high school drama clubs. So, yeah, I think acting was in my blood.

His *Star Trek* cast mate, Nichelle Nichols, who played Lt. Uhura, had the burden of representing the entire Black community in a positive light on *Star Trek*, and Takei had a similar obligation to the Asian one.

TAKEI: You have to remember back. This was the mid-1960s. Every time we had a hot war going on in Asia, it was difficult for Asian Americans here. During the Second World War, Japanese Americans were incarcerated. During the Korean War, we had a lot of depiction of Asians as villains and evil cutthroat people, and in the 1960s, we were in a war in Vietnam. On the six o'clock news, you saw people who look like me wearing black pyjamas characterized as the enemy and people we had to shoot. So, here again, the traditional war in Asia syndrome was on American television and movies, except when *Star Trek* came on. You saw another Asian face and he was one of the good guys, one of us. So, I think Sulu played a very important role in balancing the perception of Asians by the North American public.

Six years later, in another conversation with the *Star Trek* star, the topic of being a role model for Asians came up again. I informed him of a chat I had with actor Garrett Wang, who played Ensign Harry Kim on *Star Trek: Voyager* (1995). Wang confessed Takei's portrayal of Sulu was a role model for him. I wondered if Takei was aware of the imprint he had on young Asian Americans.

TAKEI: I most certainly am. So many young people have come up to me and told me that seeing Sulu on TV, playing the kind of heroic role he did, has made a world of difference to them. I also had the unique privilege of meeting Ellison Onizuka, the Japanese-American astronaut, who died in the [Space Shuttle] *Challenger* accident. He told me the same thing. When he was in college, he used to watch *Star Trek,* because, for him, it was very satisfying to see someone who looked like him on TV. And I told him he is actually going to be the ancestor of Sulu."

PETER: The show went on for three years, and then it went off. Did you feel like everyone else? Okay, that was a nice role. Three years, it's done, it's over.

TAKEI: Exactly! That happens in show business all the time. Plays close, movies wrap, and TV series eventually get cancelled, and we were cancelled in three seasons. I had predicted at best we'd probably have two seasons. I said to

Jimmy Doohan [Scotty], as a matter of fact, when we were shooting the pilot, "I smell quality with this show, and that means we're in trouble, because television doesn't respect quality." And we got one season more than I had predicted. So, I feel we were really lucky, and you just move on to the next project, and I never, ever thought we'd have this almost thirty-year phenomenon.

PETER: At what point after the cancellation of the show did you start to be aware of the fact that *Star Trek* was becoming a phenomenon?

TAKEI: I went to a convention in New York City in 1971, I think. It was a huge gathering of people. I mean, I thought, *The show's been cancelled. It's been gone for two years, it's in syndication now.* To have a convention—and they offered to pay my expenses and go to New York—and I thought, *These people are getting in over their head!* But when I arrived there and saw the huge crowd, then I realized there was something very interesting happening here.

PETER: Did you ever think after doing the convention perhaps there was a chance for Mr. Sulu to re-emerge, either on television or on the big screen, or did you think, "Oh well, now I'm just going to do some conventions and on with my acting career and other things?"

TAKEI: Exactly! I thought this convention phenomenon was very flattering, but that's about the extent of it. Then, a few years later, this effort to revive *Star Trek*, you know that slogan "*Star Trek* Lives" started to pop up. And sure enough it did revive itself in the shape of an animated cartoon series on Saturday afternoons. And I thought, *Well, that's interesting. We'll do the voices on it but nothing else will happen. We're a cancelled series and this is just a prolonged phasing out.* But ten years later, ten years after we were cancelled, we came back as a major feature motion picture. [*Star Trek The Motion Picture*, 1979.] I thought *that* would be the end of it. That's one last gasp of glory. Then, that did very well at the box office, so before you knew it, we were in a string of feature motion pictures. And then they announce they're going to do some spinoffs of us!

PETER: Through the years you've played Sulu, have you had to fight for the development of the character from the way it was written in the initial pilot?

TAKEI: *Oh yes!* In my book, I tell the twenty-five-year struggle to give Sulu something more substantial to do, and then the struggle to get a captaincy for him. As a matter of fact, in *Star Trek II: The Wrath of Khan* (1982), I was successful in getting them to write in a captaincy for Sulu, and we actually shot that scene. You'll find out in the book why that scene never made on the screen.

Takei thought it was very important to fight for the rights of his character because of the overall message *Star Trek* represents. It was a metaphor for all that was good and could be great about Earth, an idealized representation of what our planet should be.

TAKEI: In our society, we have a lot of minorities getting on the upward mobility escalator. They're making progress, but the problem seems to be that thing called "the glass ceiling." They make it up to a certain point, and then it stops. I kept lobbying to the powers that be at Paramount, saying to them, "If Starfleet is to represent that ideal, you just can't keep giving us advances in rank." By that time, I was a Commander, the movie before I was a Lt. Commander, but I was still there at the helm punching those same buttons. I said to them, "If we are supposed to be the bright, eminently capable professionals, we have to get that advancement." We have to be able to show this ideal society truly works. It's very important we see one of the characters moving up and becoming a captain, and, of course, my character being Sulu, I lobbied most vigorously for him. Finally, after twenty-five long years of lobbying, we were able to reach the idealized representation of Starfleet.

There has been a lot of documentation about some of the strong personalities within the cast of *Star Trek*, primarily Takei's sometimes contentious relationship with the Captain of the Starship Enterprise.

TAKEI: It was a very talented group of people. I know it's kind of a cliché to say this but, we really are a family. We've been together for these thirty years now, and I look forward to each one of the movies we do as something of a family reunion. But like any large extensive family there is that 'Uncle Jack' you can't stand, and we do have "Uncle Jack" in "Uncle Bill." But he is a member of the family, and you develop some kind of way of working and living with each other for the three months you're together making the film. Although I must say he does make it very difficult.

When I reminded Takei that he was talking to an audience in Montreal, the home town of William Shatner, a place where even prestigious McGill University has a William Shatner Building, Takei really saw no need to put on the brakes.

TAKEI: Well, I know that's his home town, and I know his mother lives there, and I'm sure she's a very sweet dear lady, but she has certainly given birth to a supremely self-possessed man.

While some actors harbour concerns that playing such a popular character, especially one who has gone on for more than a generation, can be stereo-typically confining, Takei feels quite the opposite. The worldwide cache of *Star Trek* made it possible for him to be cast in international productions because of the global reach *Star Trek* has. He did theater all through Britain and appeared I films in the UK and Australia.

TAKEI: If anything, *Star Trek* has opened doors that would not have been opened otherwise. It's because my name has some commercial currency. Thanks to *Star Trek*, I can sell tickets, which the other Asian actors in London cannot do. So, if anything, *Star Trek* has burnished my career opportunities. *Star Trek* fans come in every guise, shape, and form, and *Star Trek* has done wonderful things to lubricate the opening of other doors I never expected to be able to open.

To boldly go, indeed!

Alan Bean. Photo courtesy of NASA

Chapter 13

Alan Bean

There are only twelve sets of human footprints on the surface of the Moon, and I have had the pleasure of talking to two of the men who put them there. Harrison Schmitt was the last man up there, along with Eugene Cernan, in December 1972 on Apollo 17. Three years earlier, in November 1969, Alan Bean, along with Charles "Pete" Conrad, were the third and fourth humans to skip across the lunar surface as part of the Apollo 12 mission.

Thirty years later in 1999, I chatted with Bean, as he was promoting what was an absolutely marvellous and unique coffee table book, *Apollo: An Eyewitness Account By Astronaut/Explorer Artist/Moonwalker Alan Bean.* Bean also flew as the commander of the Skylab II mission, America's first space station, logging 24,400,000 miles in orbit for fifty-nine days. What made that book so special was that it was filled with artistic renderings of Bean's journey into space, and all the artwork was done by him.

Following America's journey into space, we had come to understand that the men helming the missions were pilots and engineers with military backgrounds, trained to be astronauts. Little did we know that one of them was an artist.

BEAN: Even though it was my hobby, I never thought of it as a profession. It was only after I got back from the Moon and Skylab and others, when I began to think about what might be a good thing to do next. There were many, many astronauts who could fly the space shuttle as good as I could or better, but there was no one interested in recording one of the great human adventures of all time.

In the past, when mankind chose to explore, it was always in larger groups. Ships crossed the seas with a full complement of men, which always included artists, who created renderings of the journey. In a three-man spacecraft, with only two occupants going down to the lunar surface, there wasn't a whole lot of room for an artist, but with Alan Bean, NASA got a two for one deal.

BEAN: The reason I became an astronaut really, back in 1963, was because I liked doing those things and I like the way the lunar module looked and the suits looked and felt. So, I noticed when I'm painting them I feel the same sorts of feelings going through my brain—that I like the looks of these; I like the look of the lunar dirt, things like that.

The paintings represent seventeen years of artwork that Bean created since he left the Space Program in 1981. When you consider the Moon is a grey expanse with a black sky and you have astronauts on the surface in white suits, there isn't a lot of colour to depict for an artist, whose favourite impressionist is Monet, a painter known for vivid colours. Bean didn't know if he could capture the Moon on canvas and make it beautiful.

BEAN: But I realized that was the scientist and technical observer in me talking, and as I began to paint it, I realized I could change those colours a little bit. You know, as long as it could still look like an astronaut on the Moon, I could explore some warm and cool colours, some purples and blues and reds and oranges. As long as I didn't make them too strong, it satisfied my artistic urge. So, it took a little while to realize the Moon was good raw material.

PETER: It's interesting to have a chance to talk to you because of your artistic talent and showing us a different perspective of going into space and going to the Moon. The reason I bring that up is I had the opportunity on another program to talk to Harrison Schmitt.

BEAN: Oh yeah, Jack Schmitt, a wonderful, wonderful, but a hundred percent scientist in his head.

PETER: But that's why I wanted to talk to him. I was watching, *From the Earth to the Moon,* the HBO series, and I just found fascinating the stories depicting the whole geological training they had in the desert before they went to space. I think it's a combination of learning about the science and what it took to get man to the Moon, and also looking at it from your artistic point of view, that makes it more human for the average person. I think both of them together are two points that give a reason why we should spend the money and time and do this again.

BEAN: Well, I think you're absolutely right. Jack Schmitt helped every crew; he was kind of a coordinator between the scientific community, the geologist, and the crew members. We were all test pilots and engineer types. We didn't know a lot of geology, and we didn't care about it like he did. So, he was able to kind of infuse some excitement about studying rocks and dirt and looking at topography and make it exciting to us. Not as exciting as it was to him. That's why it was so wonderful how it went, but flying was more exciting to us than it was to him, so it turned out to be a nice combination. Jack Schmitt turned out to be a great contribution to Apollo.

After the excitement of the first couple of Moon missions died down, the general population lost a bit of the enthusiasm for them. I brought up Alan Shepard's lunar golf swing during the Apollo 14 mission as something people looked back on, and Bean was quick to share his changing thoughts on that historic moment.

BEAN: When I watched Alan Shepard on Apollo 14 hit the golf ball I thought—because in my mind and mentality—I thought, *Boy he's wasting time, he should be picking up more rocks, he should be doing more geology. Here he is just hitting a golf ball.* But after a few years, I began to say, "You know, maybe we didn't do enough things on the Moon in our exploration that were just human fun things to do. In fact, if I had it to do over again and we could go back in time, Pete and I would take a football. I didn't think that when I saw Al do it. It took a number of years. We'd take the football, we'd turn the TV [cameras] on us, I'd say, "Go deep, Pete," and I'd throw him a pass, and maybe he'd punt it back. We'd get it on TV and it would be fun. Maybe the next crew would take a soccer ball and do the same thing. It would add things human beings could relate to. They were having difficulty relating to all this science and technology, because it's just complicated, that's all there is to it.

PETER: One way of relating is going through your book, looking at your artwork. I understand some of your work is on display in several places including as large murals.

BEAN: Yes, I have a couple of really wonderful murals. One of them is at Space Center Houston, which is the visitors' center for the Johnson Space Center here. And just last year I was asked to do a mural for the Astronaut Hall of Fame down at Cape Kennedy where we launch from. It's 24 feet by about 20 feet. It's the last painting in the book and it's called *Reaching for the Stars,* because I did it for all of us, because we were reaching for the stars definitely, but I did it for all the people who come to Cape Kennedy to look around, because they're reaching for their own stars, they're not going out into space. Some of them are, but most of them aren't. Most of them go back home and they're trying to be better lawyers or doctors or machinists or fathers or mothers. Many, many people are reaching for their own stars.

Being part of the second Moon mission meant having to deal with the same dangers and obstacles Apollo 11 faced, but without the same amount of fanfare through the years that followed Neil Armstrong. That was alright by Alan Bean.

BEAN: From a piloting point of view, it was just as difficult. Every astronaut wanted to be first, but we knew all along everybody couldn't be. We had to change attitudes and find a way to be satisfied with being part of that impossible dream. Even though you knew you wanted to be the star quarterback, you were happy just to be on the team.

Bean also realized there was a chance to get more work done being second. After all, the success of Armstrong's mission was merely in getting to the Moon and back alive—no small feat—but subsequent missions had more work to do.

BEAN: There is more confidence in what can be done [on the second mission], so you have more tasks to accomplish and more time to do it. We had two EVAs [Extravehicular Activity] on Apollo 12; Apollo 11 had only one. There are some benefits to not being first, but you lose the recognition or the thrill of doing something for the first time."

PETER: When you're standing on the Moon, what's it like looking back at Earth?

BEAN: Well, it's the most beautiful place you can see. Everything else looks pretty much like it does from Earth. You still can't see the planets. They look like morning stars or evening stars so you see those, the ones that are up. The Sun just seems a little brighter, because of the lack of atmosphere on the Moon. The main thing, though, is you look at the Earth and it's blue and white, and if you look away and look back at it in several hours, it's rotated and you notice the cloud patterns changed. And maybe you can see a little orange down there that suggests maybe that's a land area. Really, it's the most beautiful thing in the universe when you're standing on the Moon. It's the most beautiful thing you can see!

I was curious to know how going to the Moon had changed him and his eleven comrades. Bean didn't really believe the journey changed the astronauts, but rather revealed who they really were.

BEAN: The ones who were religious sort of became more religious," said Bean. "The ones who were non-religious became more non-religious. I noticed that in myself, too, and I noticed for me, I became a lot happier with being on Earth. I don't complain about traffic jams. I'm just glad I'm here. If it rains today, I'll be happy.

I was up in Boston just last week speaking, and it snowed in, and I heard people complaining, and I didn't even feel at all upset. I thought, *Wow, look at this white stuff coming down. Just think, on the Moon they never have any of this. They never have any weather, they never have any clouds.* We're living in the Garden of Eden. I love the Earth. I've just been glad to be a human being, an Earthling. I feel good about that every day, to tell you the truth.

PETER: Most of us will never have the opportunity to be on the Moon. You have been there and done the artwork. We can take your word for it. The pictures are beautiful, but we can't vouch for how realistic they might be. Have you spoken to the other astronauts—your fellow Moon walkers— and had a reaction from them on your artwork?

BEAN: Yes, it's kind of interesting, too. When I left the Space Program to be an artist, even though they knew it was my hobby, some of them thought I was having a midlife crisis or something. They said, "Why would a guy leave being a wonderful astronaut and go try to be a starving artist?" To half of the people, that didn't make sense, because they didn't believe being an artist was worthwhile, but the other half thought, *Maybe that would be fun to do, maybe I'll do it.* So, it was a mixed reaction when I left. Nowadays, when they've had the chance to see the art, and I'm doing something that preserves something, that's very important to all of us, probably more important than other people, because we risked our lives doing all that stuff. It was that important to us. And so, they like it. They never do criticize it. They'll look at it and say, "Well Al, you made the Moon have a lot of purples and greens in it and I don't remember that." They never say that, but, of course it's true. I didn't see any purples and greens up there. But artists are not scientists. Artists take—and it's the same way with Monet and Van Gogh and all the other artists—artists take the raw material of reality and then they do what they want with it, depending on what kind of artist they are, and make it into something else. That's the role. So, one of the things I want to do is take my experience and the experience of the other astronauts and make it as exciting and beautiful as it *felt* to us, not necessarily how it exactly looked. So, they always like them, and the more colourful I make them the more they seem to like them, even though the reality of it is it was a grey and black world, period.

Bean recognized his place in history, but he also saw the importance of the kind of work he did with his book.

BEAN: The reason I left the Space Program was to record this adventure for future generations. I'm not going to be around here another twenty years, and neither is anybody else that was there. I say, "Take every one of those books and put them in school libraries and regular libraries," because I want kids to look at those paintings and be inspired and say, "You know, when I grow up I'm going to go to the moon," or "When I grow up, I'm going to go to Mars and do some better geology than Alan Bean did."

There might indeed have been a better space traveling geologist out there, but I somehow doubted there would be someone on the Moon as artistic as Alan Bean for a myriad of generations to come.

Harrison Schmitt. Photo courtesy of NASA.

Chapter 14

Harrison Schmitt

Harrison Schmitt had been a very productive person. He earned a PhD in geology based on his geological field studies in Norway. Later in life, he entered politics, serving as a U.S. Senator representing New Mexico for six years starting in 1977. Both achievements in their own right would be considered the basis of a very successful life, but it was what Schmitt did in between those accomplishments that made him stand out. Schmitt was one of only twelve men in history who have walked on the surface of the Moon.

In December 1972, Harrison Schmitt was a member of the crew of Apollo 17, the last manned mission to the lunar surface. I was thrilled to talk to him on two separate occasions, first in June 1998, then nine years later in September 2007.

In between those conversations, I also chatted with Alan Bean, who was part of the Apollo 12 mission to the Moon in November 1969. While many touted the accomplishments of the earlier missions, starting with Neil Armstrong's historic first landing with Apollo 11, I had always been partial to Harrison Schmitt's mission.

After the airing of the 1998 HBO series, *From The Earth To The Moon*, I decided to contact Schmitt. I was fascinated with his work, because, unlike previous astronauts, Schmitt was a scientist first. He was the first from NASA's scientist-astronaut group to fly into space.

PETER: It's been such a while, over thirty years since you came back from the Moon on the December 19, 1972. Did you think, *Well, that's it, we're not going back?*

SCHMITT: Well, I knew we weren't going back with the Apollo system. That series of decisions had been made for many years, unfortunately, but I have to admit I'm a little surprised it took us so long to find a President [George W. Bush] and a Congress willing to commit to going back in the not-to-distant future and maybe sooner rather than later, depending on what happens internationally.

PETER: The shots going to the Moon in the first place seemed to be just a space race against the Soviet Union at the time.

SCHMITT: Well, it definitely was. You always have to remember the origins of Apollo lie in the Cold War. It was entirely, at least in Kennedy's mind and in Eisenhower's mind before him, a question of a space race, of being able to show the world the forces of freedom were equal to the challenge presented to them by the then Soviet Union.

While I was a staunch believer in the exploratory nature of NASA missions, there were those who wondered whether the expense of manned missions was worth the effort. I had always wanted to have that question answered by someone who could definitively state their case. Schmitt didn't let me down.

SCHMITT: Well, people who ask the question obviously are not field geologists. Field geology and field exploration has been going on now since humanity began to move out of Africa, but as a profession, has its roots in England with William Smith. That is a process by which a human being utilizes his brain, his eyes, and his hands, or her brain, eyes, and hands, to try to understand the situation in which they're placed, from the point of view of rocks and minerals and various environmental factors. It is something robots are not yet capable of doing, nor do I ever expect them to ever be able to integrate their training and experience to an instantaneous analysis of the significance of a particular situation. That's what human beings do best, and we ought to plan on utilizing them in that regard. Robots do some things very well and better than humans, particularly where it's just systematic collection of information, but when it comes to looking at a new situation and deciding what is the best way to approach that situation, and what may be its significance, it's the old characteristic of being perspicacious. That's a human characteristic, not a robotic characteristic.

With each lunar mission, the level of science increased, but Schmitt was quick to point out that the Apollo 11 crew did a remarkable geological job right out of the gate.

SCHMITT: Neil Armstrong collected one of the finest suites of samples, from a geological point of view, that anybody in the same amount of time ever collected. He is an excellent observer. He did a really remarkable job in giving us a very broad distribution of the types of samples present at Tranquility Base, the Apollo 11 landing site.

Schmitt's belief and confidence in the missions never wavered during the Apollo program, even when the harrowing circumstances of Apollo 13, following an oxygen tank explosion in space, left the lives of three astronauts, James Lovell, Jack Swigert, and Fred Haise, hanging in the balance as Mission Control tried to rescue them.

SCHMITT: My confidence was probably reinforced by two things: one is the way the overall system came together to rescue the crew and to do things with the spacecraft we never knew we could do. These spacecraft had become complex enough that, like the human body, you find it can do things you never imagined when it is tested. We found that out with Apollo 13, so it was encouraging to know the system was able to pull everything together to do what seemed initially to be impossible, namely to rescue the crew.

The other thing was in response to the accident, like all accidents in the space program, particularly what we know as the 204 fire that killed Gus Grissom and his crew [Grissom, Ed White and Roger Chaffee died during a pre-launch test for Apollo 1 in 1967], the engineers, the manufacturers, the designers, the operators, everyone took the lessons to heart and built a far better spacecraft. So, I never lost any confidence. In fact, my confidence continued to increase. Of course, I was right in the middle of all of it and I was part of doing that [rescue] response. So, one would expect I had confidence in what the teams I worked with were able to do, as well as those other teams outside my own area of responsibility.

On Apollo 17, Schmitt spent a total of just over three days on the lunar surface, along with Commander Eugene Cernan, venturing out of the Lunar Landing Module three times for eight-hour shifts, conducting experiments and collecting samples in the Taurus-Littrow Valley.

SCHMITT: It was really just a delightful time in a remarkable location on the Moon. Deep mountain valley, deeper actually than the Grand Canyon of The Colorado in Arizona; it was really one of the most beautiful places I've ever seen.

The training process for Schmitt was a long one. Before being assigned a mission, astronauts trained to be a backup to one. In Schmitt's case, he trained as a backup to James Irwin on Apollo 15.

SCHMITT: That's a very, very important part of the training. I went through about fifteen/sixteen months of training for Apollo 15, and then immediately was assigned to the Apollo 17 crew, replacing Joe Engle at the time, because it was determined by certain people in NASA, fortunately, that we ought to have a geologist go to the Moon before the end of the Apollo program.

Gearing up for his mission meant another eighteen months of prepping, on top of the regimen of initial astronaut training.

SCHMITT: Before that, of course, there's a lot of generalized training that goes on in making sure you understand the spacecraft systems, the principles of flight in space, and also you exercise an assignment in some technical area.

Schmitt's technical assignment was to oversee scientific activities of the astronauts, starting with Apollo 8, and also to oversee the final development and preparation of the descent stage of the Lunar Module where all the scientific gear was housed. One point I found surprising was the idea of the Moon as a source of energy.

PETER: From a scientific point of view, what do you think is the most important thing we learned with the flights to the Moon in general and from your specific mission, Apollo 17?

SCHMITT: Well, long-term, maybe the most important thing we learned—and we learned this initially with just the analyses of the Apollo 11 samples, although it wasn't fully recognized for about thirteen years—we learned there is an energy resource in the soils of the Moon. A light isotope of helium called Helium 3 that ultimately, I believe, will play a very, very important role as we transition away from fossil fuels here on Earth to other methods of producing electricity, in this case by fusion using lunar fuel. That will probably have the greatest long-term impact. I've written a book on the subject called, *Return to the Moon,* and it is based on the realization by engineers and scientists at the University of Wisconsin, Madison that indeed the Apollo 11 samples contained a significant concentration of this light isotope of helium. Now, scientifically, our exploration of the Moon so far has developed what one might call a first order understanding of the origin and evolution of the Moon, which in turn related directly to the first 800 million years of Earth history. Because these two bodies have been exposed to the same environment in the solar system over about four and a half billion years, and although the

Moon became relatively quiet compared to the Earth, about 3.8 billion years ago, the Earth continued to evolve, and it pretty much destroyed most of the signs of its early history. We're beginning to tease out some of those signs, primarily because the Moon has taught us where to look and how to look.

PETER: You mentioned the qualities in the samples brought back from the Moon. Are you saying the Moon could be mined for energy?

SCHMITT: Oh yes, no question about it. The pulverized upper surface of the Moon, what we call the regolith, averages in the older portions of the Moon, the older areas covered by lava flows, averages about six meters deep. Taking the area where Neil Armstrong landed for example, if one were to process about two square kilometres to a depth of three metres, you would be able to extract about 100 kilograms of Helium 3, and that fuel has so much energy content it would supply a thousand megawatt electric power plant— when we are complete designing such a thing and building it—supply that power plant for a year, actually over a year. And a thousand megawatts or a gigawatt of power is about what a city the size of Dallas, for example, uses in a year. So, it is a significant potential resource for the long-term for the Earth.

PETER: On the scarier side of things, could it also be used in weaponry?

SCHMITT: No. It turns out Helium 3, one of the great advantages of Helium 3 fusion is, first of all, Helium 3 is not radioactive. Second of all, it does not produce radioactive materials. It produces a proton rather than a neutron, and it's not the kind of process that can be used really to manufacture weapons-grade material.

PETER: We have this romantic idea of the Moon. Songs are written about it, and poems are written about it, but you're only one of twelve people to actually walk up there. When you look up at it at night, what do you think?

SCHMITT: Well, it sort of depends on who I'm with, Peter (laughter).

Most of the time, I'm with my wife, and it's just a very delightful thing to be able to look up at the Moon. I have to say it catches my eye more than it did before I went. I have some delightful memories of my experiences. I feel very honoured and privileged to have been in a position to actually go to the Moon and to contribute both scientifically and to the needs of America in the process.

As with my conversation with Alan Bean, I was curious as to whether the experience of being in the so-called "Heavens" changed him in any way spiritually.

SCHMITT: My observation is all of the astronauts—and you'd have to talk to each one of them individually—found their beliefs reinforced. I found in addition I gained a great deal of confidence in what human beings can do, particularly young human beings, when they're motivated to take on a very complex and demanding task. If they believe in that task, if they believe it's worth doing, then nothing is impossible within the limits of technology that can be reached during the period of time the task takes.

Schmitt believed in what later became an adage.

SCHMIT: The old question of if you can go to the Moon, why can't you, and then fill in the blank, is you have to be motivated to fill in the blank. And if you are, particularly if you have young men and women to do it, who have the stamina, imagination, as well as the motivation to undertake those kinds of tasks, well we can take care of essentially anything we have to.

Being one of only a dozen men to walk on the Moon was pretty heady stuff. You might think the experience would make life after the journey pale in comparison, but not for Schmitt.

SCHMITT: My life has been a fortunate journey. I feel very fortunate to have had all the opportunities I've had. Of course, as soon as I came back, I began to work scientifically on the materials and information gathered during Apollo. I had been interested in politics for many, many years beginning with my graduate work at Harvard, and so I began to look seriously at getting involved in elected politics. So, I've just never had a chance to slow down to start to make comparisons.

A field geologist, Senator, and one of the few men to have walked on the Moon, Harrison Schmitt was a fascinating human being, who was remarkably down to Earth.

Chapter 15

The Milton Berle Bet

T hey don't make them like they used to." People of a certain age were prone to use that mantra when discussing a variety of things from tangible items, such as appliances and automobiles, to creative art forms, such as paintings, films, theater, and literature, and even to a generation of human beings, who were thought to possess qualities of strength, honour, or professionalism. It could also apply to Milton Berle.

Known as "Uncle Miltie," "Mr. Television," or "The Thief of Bad Gags," Milton Berle was America's first television star. He was a staple on U.S. TV screens during the medium's earliest days, hosting NBC's *Texaco Star Theater* from 1948 to 1955, yet he started entertaining as a child in Vaudeville, and he was also a true professional.

I was able to witness that first hand one Saturday night in July 1991, when the comedy legend was performing at Montreal's Just for Laughs International Comedy Festival. The eighty-three-year-old Berle was to be honoured as the first inductee into the newly minted Just for Laughs Comedy Hall of Fame. He was also performing at the festival in several shows, including a live television broadcast via the cable network, Showtime.

I was backstage for the show, which featured the talents of Jane Curtin, Kevin Nealon, and Mark Schiff, to name a few, and hosted by Mary Tyler

Moore. The night before, the same line up took to the stage in front of a packed house at Theatre St. Denis, which gave the Showtime crew a dry run at camera blocking and timing for the live broadcast the next night.

Everyone had a set time for their act, and Milton Berle was the closer. He was scheduled to do nine minutes. On the Friday night show, Berle took to the stage and did what he did best. He had the audience in stitches. Only problem was, that stitching took seventeen minutes, almost twice the allotted time for the comedian.

While the audience loved it, director Paul Miller and the crew in the Showtime truck were fit to be tied. Stellar as the performance was, if Milton was to go that long on the live broadcast, it would mean a show going well over time, and thanks to satellite feed rates, well over budget. Since Berle was the closing act, there was nothing they could cut out after.

This was a cause for concern, and word soon spread that Berle could be a problem on the Saturday night show. At eighty-three, did he lose his television chops, or was this just an old man in the twilight of his career who didn't care about the show around him, but rather just wanted to soak up the audience's laughter a little bit more? No one really knew, but comedians being comedians, many were willing to bet on it.

On Saturday night, a pool was started, and comics who weren't even on the bill got involved in the betting. The range of guesses ran from conservatively under the allotted time on stage to liberally well over it, and the pot had grown to north of $300.

I remember comic Richard Belzer putting in his bet and saying, "Berle is a professional. It doesn't matter what he did last night. The cameras are rolling tonight. If he's supposed to do nine minutes, he'll do nine.

The moment of truth was upon us. Many of us were backstage as a crowd gathered around a small television on a stand that offered a feed of the show from the truck outside. Performers, crew, and assorted "suits" stared at the screen as if they were watching Neil Armstrong's first steps on the moon. Someone had a stopwatch, and we heard the click as Berle uttered his first words to yet another adoring audience.

One of the comics blurted out, "He's not even doing the same jokes he did last night! This is a different routine!"

Murmurs of acknowledgement went through the small mob, many speculating if this could mean Uncle Miltie could go even longer. We imagined director Paul Miller in the truck having heart palpitations wondering where this was headed.

When Berle told his last joke, the stopwatch clicked again. Nine minutes! Although many had doubted, Berle knew how to tell time, and Belzer knew how to bet wisely. The one thing no one ever doubted was that Milton Berle could tell a joke. What they might not have known was that he could also pull off a joke offstage, as well. Before the show started, Berle had placed his own bet in the pool, predicting a time of 19 minutes, and he made sure somehow that word of his own wager would get back to those in the truck. Classic comedy . . . indeed, they really don't make them like that anymore.

Chapter 16

A Tale of Two Celebrities —
Lynn Johnston and Ivan Reitman

In summer 1996, my duties at Montreal's international comedy festival, Just for Laughs (JFL), included co-producing two tribute shows honouring two Canadians known for making people laugh: Lynn Johnston, creator of the syndicated comic strip, *For Better Or For Worse*, which was seen in 2,000 newspapers in Canada, the United States, and twenty other countries, and film producer and director Ivan Reitman, best-known for such hit films as *Ghostbusters* (1984), *Stripes* (1981), and *Kindergarten Cop* (1990), to name a few.

The focus of the shows would be conversations with both individuals in the quaint 400-seat Gesu Theatre, where the audience could ask questions. Two years previous to this event, I hosted two tribute shows honouring *The Brady Bunch* and *Gilligan's Island* creator, Sherwood Schwartz. Since I was producing this time, I thought a different format, where I wasn't required to host and moderate, would be best.

The two shows were mounted on the same day. Lynn Johnston had the house for a late afternoon, while Ivan Reitman had the evening. My co-producer for the event was Steven Paul Leiva, a writer and animation producer

I met at the festival six years earlier. We had become fast friends (and still were years later). He had been the president of Chuck Jones Productions and produced the animation for the Ivan Reitman produced film, *Space Jam* (1996) that featured Michael Jordan and a host of Looney Tunes characters.

The programs were several months in the planning. Since Steve was in Los Angeles, he got to do all the heavy lifting, along with the JFL crew, when it came to putting together the Reitman show, while I handled Johnston and her needs here in Canada. The only real dealings I had with the Reitman crew were in the days leading up to the show. The difference between the Reitman camp and the Johnston camp were like night and day.

In my capacity, I didn't have to deal with the contracts involved for the performers, but I did have a budget for mounting the shows and was determined to spend it. The only problem was that I was trying to spend it on Lynn Johnston. When it comes to the needs of performers there are those who are known as divas or prima donnas. Go ahead and try to find antonyms for either one of those words. There is no opposite, so let's just coin one now; the hyphenated word "Lynn-Johnston."

Almost every attempt made to spend money on her, she hemmed and hawed or outright rebuffed. The show was to feature some of her artwork on display, both in the halls of the theater and in a side room, where she would sign autographs later. An overhead projector was required so she could draw on stage as she chatted in a one-woman-style show.

Springing for the overhead projector, table, chairs, and markers was the easy part, but when it came to her artwork, she said, "Where do you want me to courier the items to you after I get them mounted?"

I tried to explain to her this was my problem and all she had to do was let us know when and where we could pick them up, at our expense, and we would have them mounted and framed professionally. This was one of many examples of when I had to repeat to her what became my mantra of, "Lynn, we have a budget to spend on you. Please let me use it."

On the day of the show, at my anal retentive best, I was trying to make sure every "t" was crossed and every "i" dotted. It was key to have everything and everyone in their places well before show time, just to be safe.

The hotel Lynn and her daughter were staying at was about a ten-minute drive from the theater. It was a hot, sticky July day. A car was sent to the hotel well in advance, so Lynn would arrive in air conditioned splendour, ready for the afternoon show.

Imagine my surprise when the driver got to the hotel and there was no sign of Lynn Johnston. The show was about an hour away, but my heartbeat was now thundering in my ears. Phone calls were made to the room, to the desk, but no sign of Lynn. The car service was called to make sure they had the right location and a check to see if perhaps she went with another driver. No such luck. About fifteen minutes later, who do I see walking toward the theater? Lynn Johnston and her daughter, both with the wide-eyed look of contented tourists.

"What a gorgeous day!" she bellowed. "Katie and I thought we'd walk here from the hotel. Beautiful city you have here!"

All I could do was laugh. Later, she did her show, enthralling the audience with witty story after story about how she became the beloved cartoonist we all knew. She had the audience in the palm of her hand while she did free-style drawings on the overhead projector. It was a marvellous experience.

After the event, she graciously signed autographs in the side room. With many in the audience wanting to get her signature and chat one-on-one, the room started to get just a little sticky with the added body heat in such a small place. Wanting to make sure she was comfortable, and also wanting to get as many people out of the room so we could clear the house and prepare for the second show, I suggested to her that we cut this short. Lynn was in her element. She just wanted to talk to her fans and have a little fun. They loved her, and she definitely loved them. The room was warm, but it wasn't just the temperature.

I was beginning to think, heart palpitations aside, that there wasn't too much to this producing gig. The first show had gone off without a hitch, so upward and onward to Ivan Reitman, but the Devil is in the details and Satan had a clipboard.

I never really got to speak one on one with Ivan, because, unlike Lynn, he had people—people who wanted to have hotel suites changed in a hotel that was already overbooked; people who wanted guarantees about the use of a studio jet; people who wanted an entire section of the theater roped off for VIPs; people who needed to pester other people, mainly me.

Reitman's show was hosted, at his request, by one of his old pals, Len Blum, who co-wrote the script for *Meatballs*. In hindsight, I'm fully aware that someone who has a soft, wispy voice might not be the best person to host in a 400-seat theater. Microphones can only do so much. I remember actually going on stage because I thought there was a problem with Len's mic. I replaced the one attached to his lapel, giving him a hand-held. No difference.

I won't necessarily characterize the night as a disaster, but I can't really call it a stellar one. Perhaps it was all the hassle leading up to it that dampened my enthusiasm. How I wished I could have batted a thousand after doing so well earlier in the day with the delightful Lynn Johnston.

When the festival was all over, I put the players of the day behind me. I never heard from Ivan Reitman or his people again, but I did hear from Lynn Johnston. She sent me a note (see illustration).

It was indeed a day that was for better and for worse, and I was better for it, for having met Lynn Johnston.

Aug 3/96

Dear Peter

I just wanted to thank you again for your hospitality, your support & your kind introduction. The T.F.L. fest was a wonderful world for me – and to have been honored by this assoc. was an overwhelming event in my life. I'll take that award to the crypt with me!

I hope our paths cross again & I wish you well with your work. You're great company!

Sincerely

CONTACT: UNIVERSAL PRESS SYNDICATE, 4900 MAIN ST, KANSAS CITY, MO., 64112

Letter from Lynn Johnston (Aug 1996).

Chapter 17

Tom Arnold

om Arnold has had a full career, both as an actor and a comic. When I caught up with him in July 2010, he was headlining a show at Montreal's Just for Laughs Comedy Festival. By then, he had already starred in over seventy movies, been the lead in his own sitcom, a regular on several others, and had toured large venues as a comic, yet he never seemed to get the respect that a man of his accomplishments and talent deserved, which was a shame considering that he was the kind of personality, perhaps to a fault, who worked overtime to be accepted.

Our encounter was such an example. I was the live, backstage announcer at a venue where he was performing. Since I always did double duty, taking my vacation to work there while recording audio interviews for after the fest, I asked Arnold if he would sit down for a chat.

I wanted about fifteen minutes of his time, but he was doing two shows nightly, and it was tight. However, eager-to-please-Tom went out of his way to be accommodating. That was why, in between two shows during a dinner break, we found ourselves in the bowels of Club Soda underneath the stage having a conversation.

By this time, I had spent several days in his company, witnessing his interactions with everyone. He was always concerned about whether he was doing everything he needed to make the show work and checking in with other performers and crew to see if they were okay.

I asked him about the beating he got in the media and online and the lack of acknowledgement that hovered over him.

ARNOLD: I feel like sometimes I overdo it, and people are like, "Why would you do it, why do you care? Don't Google your name. Don't pay attention to critics. You've had enough."

Despite the outpouring of negativity, Arnold felt very blessed in his career. Before he broke into show business, he worked for three years at a meat packing company, so he knew he had come far in life. Yet, he admitted that he often took what others said too much to heart.

ARNOLD: I remember once there was this kid who had a website called "Tom Arnold is the Devil," and I read about it and ended up contacting this person. It turned out to be a kid who was twenty-two, and lived in his mother's basement, and he had no friends until he had this website. And now, he had about 200 friends, and I felt so bad about it. This guy out of nowhere was trying to have a little fun, and I should be able to take it. That's part of the job. And so, I was crushing him. So, I said, "Put the site back, in fact I'll give you some stuff proving I am the devil!" So, I always regret when I do something or say something because it always makes me look like an ass.

Throughout the conversation Arnold not only constantly professed the luck of his career, he often apologized for things that he has no need to apologize for. I called him on it, reminding him you have to be good to succeed in some of the roles he had, such as his dramatic turn in *True Lies* (1994).

ARNOLD: *True Lies* is a big Hollywood movie that came out right when my first divorce [to Rosanne Barr], a very public, ugly mess, where people said I'll never work again. And then this movie comes out that I've been working on for a year, and people in Hollywood who didn't even know me went, "Oh, maybe he is a decent guy." Not that they ever met me, but I was good in a good movie.

Arnold's need-to-please personality meant he couldn't say no to work, even if the project wasn't a top shelf one. That led to forgettable movie roles and more knocks on his career. He has had to start over several times, appearing in independent features, working his craft. His biggest fear was not being taken seriously.

ARNOLD: The first time I did a serious movie was a film Steve Buscemi directed called *Animal Factory* (2000), with Steve, Mickey Rourke, Willem Defoe, and a whole bunch of people. It was based in a prison. My fear was people would come to the screening, see me come on as this prison rapist, and then start laughing. I got lucky and they accepted me as a prison rapist, which I guess also is not a great compliment, but I got to work with these great actors in this little movie.

Arnold realized early in his career that he wasn't going to have the slow road to recognition most people have in the business. Through the course of our conversation, he referred to his first wife, Rosanne Barr, but never mentioned her name. He saw how her career got to build, unlike his own, which, thanks to the marriage, burst onto the scene.

ARNOLD: My first wife, I knew her before she was famous, I knew her when she was coming up. I knew how talented she was, and as her friend, it was just so awesome to be a part of that, write a joke or two for her, and watch her rise. Then, she went on *The Tonight Show*, that was her big coming out, and [Johnny Carson] called her over. And I realized once I got married to a famous person I would never have a coming out. You were tainted in a way. You were already famous.

Arnold accepted the changes in his life, because the upside was he had an instant family with a wife and stepchildren, but he recognized how different his coming out was in a role he had opposite Dustin Hoffman in the 1992 film *Hero*.

ARNOLD: We went to the movies, and they had the coming attraction to this movie, *Hero*. I was only in five scenes, but that was pretty much the whole preview. I'm sitting there in the theater with my stepkids and my wife and looking around thinking, *Well, this is my moment.* Maybe it's not with Johnny Carson, like most comedians dream of, but maybe this is how my life goes.

PETER: With all you've done, again over seventy movies, several television shows, now doing stand-up comedy, is there something in your career you want to do, but you haven't had the chance to?

ARNOLD: Well, I'm getting ready to do an hour long stand-up special. I've done three *HBO* specials awhile back, but it wasn't stand-up related. It was based on bits and chunks and it was actually Judd Apatow's first job ever. I had hired him, I had seen him. I found a lot of guys through stand-up comedy who became writers. I guess I'm proudest of the fact I could recognize talent in others. I would staff *The Roseanne Show* and *Jackie Thomas* and these other shows I did based on if I see good comics and I'd say, "I could teach you how to write the two act television script. I can't teach you how to be funny." And so a lot of people got their start via me. It made me look good, obviously, but that's one of the things I'm proudest of. There are comics here who have won Emmys and stuff. I saw them on stage and said, "I know this guy's funny. I know they can write. He's gonna make me look good. Bring him on. Teach him this little form we use. The thing about comics you have to remember is you always have to have a couple of old timers with them because you have to make sure the scripts are done on Thursday. You gotta have it done. A lot of guys got their start that way. You know, people have been very kind to me, too, so, you know I always feel like I wish I was in a clique with all the cool kids, but for as lucky as I've been I wouldn't trade anything.

PETER: Talking about the cliques, in your stand-up routine, you talk about working on films, and the idea it's a camaraderie, and you're friends with those you're on screen with. You also mention you're a good friend with the Governor of California, whom you've also worked with in a film. It sounds like one of the things you truly enjoy besides the work itself is the camaraderie and friendships that come with working in this business.

ARNOLD: Yeah, I've got a core group of guys I've been friends with for twenty years. Every once in a while, I'll meet somebody and eventually get to know them. They've been very supportive of me. They're true friends, especially when you're down. It's mostly about that. It's not about being in their movies or working together. It's about when you're down, or they need help with a charity, or you need help with a charity, or whatever. Arnold [Schwarzenegger] is a good example. He taught me the importance of charity work. He said, "If my agent doesn't know my charity work as much as he knows my movies, then he's gone." He also said, "The only reason to have an agent is so there's one person in town who isn't badmouthing you all the time." I saw the joy early on, in the late 1980s when I got to know him, that he got from doing his stuff. I would say honestly my greatest joy in life are the times when I'm at my kids' camp, or I'm doing this or that, because I'm not thinking about me, or what job I'm going to do.

Tom Arnold took the advice of Arnold Schwarzenegger literally to heart. He was involved in many charities, including Camp del Corazon, a non-profit providing free of charge, medically supervised summer camp for children with heart disease, ages seven to seventeen.

ARNOLD: Playing with the kids and having fun, it's not about me; it's also very inspirational when a kid who's had two heart transplants, and is only seven years old, is climbing the rock wall before me, or kayaking, and just living in the moment."

Arnold should have taken his own advice about living in the moment, but he often came back to his public persona.

ARNOLD: I worry about things that are so stupid sometimes. People make a lot of jokes and have a lot of fun at my expense, but the flipside is if I wasn't so well-known, they couldn't make those remarks.

He went on to tell the story of doing a table read, where actors sit around a table and read a script out loud among themselves, for a film with Tom Cruise and Will Smith.

ARNOLD: To me, that's a big honour. That's like playing with the cool kids. Will Smith is producing it, and they had a bunch of big actors there. After this table read, paparazzi were outside filming. They were calling it a Scientology meeting and whatever. I just thought to myself, *There's nobody nicer than Tom Cruise and Will Smith. People are trying to make something weird out of this.* I also thought, *If I was Tom Cruise, being a comedian, I would use all that material. I would not let people make snarky remarks. I would take a hold of it.* My goal is when I hear people make fun of me, I think, *Why didn't I think of that? Why didn't I get the joke?*

I had to give him my assessment of his personality.

PETER: I hope you don't take this the wrong way, but I've been watching you on stage for the last couple of days here in Montreal. I've seen you interact with the comics backstage, seen you interact with the crew, and with the people who work here. I don't know if you've seen the movie *Up* (2009). There is the dog in *Up* who just wants to please, who just wants the friendship of the people around him, and that's what I see in you. You seem like the happiest person when you're on stage, and I think that's a joy, not just for yourself, but the audience gets it, too. So, on behalf of the audience, I'd like to thank you for all you've done.

ARNOLD: When I'm bonding with the audience, it's real. I feel like I owe them. When I started touring a year ago, the fact they would spend their hard earned money to see me, you know, just freaks me out. So, of course, I'm going to stay around and hang out, and I think the good news and the bad news is I'm not Tom Hanks or Tom Cruise. I mean, if you saw them in an airport you would be like, "Oh my God!" But if a person sees me, it's like, "Oh my God, it's my cousin Tom Arnold. I've gotta go up and punch him in the arm and talk." So, there's definitely a connection that he's one of us, and that's all I ever want. To be able to tell stories from an outsider's perspective is what I do in my act, because people know my history. I can't lie and say I just got married for the first time and whatever is going on. I just talk about my mistakes and my positives. I sense the people are genuinely happy I'm in a good marriage. They are happy I'm not a jerk towards my [three] ex-wives; I have some gratitude for everything that's happened. I think it gives people a relief.

You could start a drinking game for the amount of times Arnold genuinely professed his luck and gratitude, but then you'd need a 12-step program. Even in saying our goodbyes in the interview, he was still giving thanks.

ARNOLD: It's been great working with you at this festival. You've made it a lot better for me and thank you very much.

No, Tom, thank you!

Chapter 18

Jerry Orbach

Montreal's annual Just For Laughs international comedy festival was not only a showcase where great talent was seen on stage, it was also a tourist attraction, bringing comedy fans from all over the world. Often, the tourists themselves were celebrities.

Such was the case in 1997, when Broadway, film, and television star, Jerry Orbach, came into town just to get a laugh or two. He was best known for his long-running role as Lennie Briscoe on the hit NBC series, *Law & Order* (1999), plus he was the guy who actually did put Baby in a corner in *Dirty Dancing* (1987).

Before and after comedy shows, the place to hang out at the festival was the Delta Hotel Bar, the event's nerve center for many years. (Actually, it was probably the place where some people also went to numb their nerves). It was packed with performers, managers, agents, TV and film executives, and media. We couldn't turn around without bumping into someone famous. In fact, we couldn't turn around, period. Sometimes, it seemed the easiest way to get out of the room was to crowd surf, mosh pit-style.

Orbach was with his wife at one of the tall circular tables near the windows, having a drink and sharing a laugh with some entertainment "suits." I walked up to him, introduced myself, and asked if I could have about fifteen minutes of his time to do a quick radio interview for later use. He graciously agreed, so over the din of the crowd, we talked about his career.

Law & Order had already been on the air for seven years at the time of our chat. Jerry credited the success of the show with the quality of the writing and even the turnover of regulars that kept the series fresh. I asked if another aspect to its uniqueness was it was shot in New York City, to which he agreed.

He said the pace of shooting in New York was faster, plus having the city as a backdrop was a bonus.

ORBACH: The talent pool of the actors we draw on as our character people. If you look at something like *NYPD Blue* (1993), which I love, I love Dennis Franz and Jimmy Smits who are terrific, but you see them walk down a New York street and then turn and walk into a building. And once they're inside the building, they're in Los Angeles. Or they drive, we call them "drive-ups" and "walk-ins." So, they shoot a week's worth of those and they have their New York background for the season, but they don't have the New York actors we get off the street almost, the gritty look of some people. It's hard to say, but there is an ethnicity about it too, you know. If we have a Puerto Rican drug dealer, and they have a Puerto Rican drug dealer, theirs is really a Mexican (laughter). Everything is just a little different, but New York is the greatest backdrop in the world.

PETER: As an actor, when you're working on location, is it a different situation when working in New York? Everything shoots in Los Angeles, and they're used to seeing crews on the road and they're kind of blasé about it, but it's not an everyday occurrence in New York, although you guys have been there for quite a few years, and shows like *New York Undercover* (1994) have been there for a few years.

ORBACH: Actually, New Yorkers are used to filming on the streets and they tend to be cooperative, although we've had people walk right between us on the sidewalk in the middle of a take, completely unaware of what's going on. But [co-star] Benjamin Bratt calls me "The King," because it's not that I know everybody in New York, but I've been there a long time and any neighbourhood we go into the restaurateurs and shopkeepers and everybody say, "Oh Jerry, how are you doing?" It's sort of the world is at your feet. It's a very pleasant way to work.

Orbach's professional career began on the New York stage, where he created the role of El Gallo back in 1960 in the original off-Broadway run of *The Fantasticks*. He was also a star on Broadway in such musicals as *Chicago* (1975), *Guys & Dolls* (1965), and *42nd Street* (1980). He also won a Tony Award for *Promises, Promises* (1968).

Yet in film, besides playing Lumière in the animated Disney musical, *Beauty & The Beast* (1991), his big screen roles tended to lean towards the dramatic, such as *Prince of the City* (1981), *Crimes and Misdemeanors* (1989), and *Dirty Dancing* (1987). This versatile actor had a habit of bouncing back from comedy to drama to musical with relative ease, but it wasn't always been easy convincing producers and directors of what he could do.

ORBACH: They pigeonhole you. They say, "He's a song and dance man. He does musicals." Then, I did a film called *Prince of the City* for Sidney Lumet, and then I started doing cops and gangsters like *F/X* (1986), so then they said, "He's a dramatic actor, he's not funny." Then, I do some comedy, or Lumière, or something like that, and they say, "Oh, he's this and he's that." At some point, I was the song and dance guy, and they said, "He doesn't do straight acting." Then, I was the dramatic heavy actor, and they said, "Well, he's not funny." And then, I was saying to another guy the other day, [Steven] Bochco was doing a thing called *Cop Rock* (1990), where the cops sang, and somebody suggested me for it, and they said, "Oh, we love his work. Does he sing?" So, you get from one pigeonhole to another and you have to keep reinventing yourself.

I was curious to know, with all he had done in a career that had such variety for almost four decades, if he was a casting director, what role he would submit himself for.

ORBACH: If it was me, I'd say Rhett Butler in the new *Gone with the Wind*. I don't know, I mean give me the best role you could think of. My thing has always been what we used to call just acting. Now it's called character acting. I just did a little movie with Al Pacino called *Chinese Coffee* (2000), where I'll be doing something nobody's ever seen me do, which I love. He's a raging intellectual, who uses extremely flowery language, and is a bitter critic of writers that I've never done anything like, but I'm capable of doing. That's the way I came up, the way I learned. I did Shakespeare, I did Chekhov and Ibsen and Shaw, and everything. That's fun for me, to recreate myself; do different characters; be different people.

What was also fun for him was the pride "New York's finest" had in watching Lennie Briscoe capture the bad guys each week.

ORBACH: For about thirty years, I've known a lot of detectives, a lot of cops and of course the reaction from them is probably the best part, the greatest reward for this type of show. Where the cops on the street say, "Hey, keep making us look good," which is, to me, the highest form of flattery.

PETER: The show has been successful for so long and there's a realism and grit to it, but the one thing I often hear about the show, even in interviews with other actors from it, is you don't get much texture from the regular characters. It's more about the work and the case involved. Does that make it a little difficult from an actor's point of view?

ORBACH: It does. I think it's not as rewarding for us in terms of Emmy nominations. We don't get to be very emotional. I try to inject a little humour into the proceedings, and once in awhile we get touched or moved by something, when the scripts allow us to. But it is a little cut and dried, but that's the way police work is. And as long as we're true to it, you know, basically we're saying, "What colour was the car, how many people were there, what time did he leave, did you ever hear them argue before?" all those kind of questions. That's what we have to do, otherwise the damn thing is going to get mired down in, "Who did you sleep with last night?" and "did you get drunk?" and that's not what our show is about.

PETER: We know a little bit about Lennie. We know he's a recovering alcoholic and he's been married several times, but since we don't know a lot about him, do you as an actor have to create in your mind what Lennie's background is to play him, or is that not even important?

ORBACH: Oh, I've created a background for him. Lennie has a background in my head and only occasionally does it surface, like when my daughter showed up last year. There'll be some personal things sneaking in a little bit here and there.

PETER: There have been constant cast changes over the years on *Law & Order.* You came into the show, not in the first year, but years later. Was it a warm welcome from the cast and crew when you arrived and what's it like as a veteran of the show when someone new shows up?

ORBACH: It's a very warm welcome. They don't stand by and wait to see if they're going to like you; the *want* to like you. It's a team, first of all. Nobody's just out for themselves because if you are you'll get buried! You've got to be helping each other out and I had the warmest kind of welcome right from the beginning. That's the way it's gotta be on something like this, where you work twelve-hour days and sometime they go to fifteen, sixteen on a Friday night. You better like each other (laughter)!

Who could not like Jerry Orbach? He was such a warm and approachable guy. We could have talked all night, but at that point, he seemed to be getting the signal from his wife that perhaps this conversation should be wrapping up. That was fine by me, because it was the highest form of flattery that Jerry Orbach would come to my city to enjoy some of the best comedy collected in one spot and also to be gracious enough to share some of his personality while hanging out in a crowded smoky bar.

Chapter 19

Michael Moriarty

O ne of the original stars of NBC's *Law & Order* was an actor at the center of the "Law" part. Michael Moriarty played liberal-leaning, strait-
laced, button-downed Assistant District Attorney Ben Stone during the first
four seasons of the long-running series. He left the show in 1994, and two
years later, he left the United States over what he deemed the attempted cen-
sorship of television by U.S. Attorney General Janet Reno.

The jazz musician, poet, and Tony Award- and Emmy Award-winning actor
moved up north to Canada, where he continued to act and win accolades,
proudly touting his Gemini Award nominations for his work in Canadian
television. He also continued to voice his conservative political views. In a
quote from a Canadian Press story, Moriarty claimed he wanted to become
the leader of Canada's right-leaning Reform Party saying, "I think [Reform
leader] Preston Manning took the party as far as he can. They need a great
communicator, and I could turn out to be the Canadian Ronald Reagan."

In March 1999, Moriarty was in Montreal working on the sci-fi television
series, *The Secret Adventures of Jules Verne* (2000). I had wanted to get him
into studio for a live interview, but our schedules couldn't successfully mesh.
It was determined the best chance to get together would be if, on a night off,
I would pick him up, bring him to the station, record the interview for future
use, and drop him back at his hotel.

Since my plan was to head out for a night on the town with my best friend, Mario Leblanc, I thought we would pick up Moriarty, do the interview, deposit him back, and be on our way. It would all be very simple.

Pulling up to the hotel, we caught a glimpse of Moriarty standing at the top of a short landing. He didn't look like the three-piece suited, short haired Ben Stone we had grown accustomed to on *Law & Order*. Instead, he was slightly dishevelled, bearded, and holding a coffee in his hands. After rolling down the window and calling his name, he stepped forward and got into the front seat, as Mario moved to the back.

Besides his appearance, the other oddity we noticed was his coffee: he didn't have a takeout cup. Instead, he had a cup and saucer, emblazoned with the hotel's logo, complete with spoon. As we drove to the station, (very slowly to avoid having him spill his brew), I asked if he missed being on *Law & Order* and if he had watch the performance of Sam Waterston, his replacement on the show. That was one of the first things to set him off. He went on about the producers of the show, how they caved in to political pressure, and how Waterston, whose character road a motorcycle, was brought in to be a sex symbol to appeal to female viewers. All the while, he gesticulated with the coffee cup.

Some of what he was saying seemed, frankly, like disjointed ramblings. As we pulled into the underground parking of the building housing the radio station, I had a brief thought of gratitude for having my friend Mario, who was actually a police officer, with me for the ride. Perhaps I had seen too many movies, where something nefarious happened to people in parking structures.

Once in the studio, Moriarty appeared to turn on the charm and an acting light switch and focused on the task at hand, but even in the introduction, he was compelled to jump in.

PETER: In studio, we have actor Michael Moriarty. He is an Emmy-winning actor—

MORIARTY: —and a Gemini. Three times! That's very important. How can Canadians put down their own awards? I, in one year, got three Gemini nominations, and when I try to bring it up, people treat it as if I caught a cold. I think that's important! Unprecedented! Three Gemini nominations in one year, three different roles. Canada, get proud!

PETER: Don't you just love new Canadians, folks. They're always so—

MORIARTY: —so humble (laughter)!

Moriarty had a prestigious career before *Law & Order* brought him household recognition. He starred in the 1973 film, *Bang the Drum Slowly,* with Robert De Niro. That same year on TV, he earned an Emmy starring opposite Katherine Hepburn in *The Glass Menagerie.* The following year saw him earn a Tony Award in the play, *Find Your Way Home.* His 88 episodes as Ben Stone brought him fame.

MORIARTY: I really wasn't famous until the [*Law & Order*] reruns on A&E. Everyone thinks I'm Ben Stone and they really have to get over it. That's kind of a disappointment to Canadians. They come up to me and say, "Oh, you're Ben Stone. I really like Ben Stone." And I tell them I'm Michael Moriarty, there really is a difference.

PETER: What is the difference between Ben Stone and Michael Moriarty?

MORIARTY: Well, there's a huge difference. I never was a lawyer. I could not be a lawyer. Maybe that's why I quit the show. To be a lawyer is to eventually be a Devil's advocate. There are certain things you have to do that you lose your soul for to do. Law is very tempting and very dangerous, I think, to the soul.

PETER: The fact that you played a lawyer brought a certain morality to Ben Stone, his personality, and his values.

MORIARTY: That was mine, and the longer the show went on, [Executive Producer] Dick Wolf and I would have fights, and I'd say, "No, Ben Stone wouldn't do this," and he'd say, "Alright what would he do?" And I'd pretty much do what I said he'd do.

PETER: Is that part of Ben Stone you?

MORIARTY: That part of Ben Stone is me, yes, my own personal idea of right and wrong. That always came through, and Dick even said, "Mike, you're the conscience of the show."

By the fourth year into the series, Moriarty's conscience got the better of him. He was battling the network, battling the government, and battling the U.S. justice system for what he called the "political football" of blaming TV for violence in America. Through his fight, he began to feel there were people at the top whom he didn't want to live with or deal with anymore, and he wanted to go from job to job rather than stay in a political situation he couldn't endure.

PETER: I know U.S. Attorney General, Janet Reno, is not one of your biggest fans.

MORIARTY: (Laughter.) Well actually, I have to thank her. You are defined best by your enemies, not your friends. Your enemies tell you who you are. Another phrase is a mongoose doesn't know he's a mongoose until he meets a snake—and I didn't know I was a fighting lonely mongoose until I met a snake—and her name was Janet Reno.

In 1993, Reno warned she would create laws to cut down on television violence if the industry didn't voluntarily do so. Moriarty threatened a lawsuit against Reno, and then became embroiled in fights with his own employers after they didn't back his idea of a lawsuit and for not taking Reno's threats seriously.

The fight became a "he said-he said" debate between Moriarty and Dick Wolf, with stories of Moriarty claiming he quit and Wolf saying he was fired for erratic behaviour.

PETER: You left *Law & Order*, you left the United States. In a battle for your principles, isn't that like letting them win?

MORIARTY: Well yes, yes, but as somebody once said—whom I cannot recall—it could be considered a strategic retreat. The issue is still there, but in the case of an administration I'm not a fan of—even though I have awful feelings about Janet Reno—I have deeper, more profound resentful feelings about the Clinton Administration. Right now, because things seem so rosy down there, I think it's full of lies, and things are going to fall apart, and so I'm waiting, and I sit, and I'm very happy up here. Down there, I get very angry, because then I'm in the midst of my own people, who have their heads planted squarely in the wrong place.

Moriarty went on to wax poetically about his newly adopted country, espousing the marriage of our two founding cultures of French and English, the success of this duality, and the personality of the country as a whole. When I pointed out the grass isn't always greener on the other side, Moriarty admitted he did have some pains about Canada, but he adopted the stance of Voltaire, the man he professes to be his favourite Frenchman.

MORIARTY: Voltaire was in exile his entire life. He was kicked out of France, then he went to Germany and he was kicked out of Germany, so his life was a sense of exile. And then, they finally begged him to come back to France, and he came back. So, I feel the place I'm in, if I love the people there, I'll stay, and if they love me and I have friends, I'll stay, and if I lose that, then I'll go to another country.

PETER: Do you anticipate, like Voltaire, the United States will ask you back?

MORIARTY: I would hope in the end, when the truth starts falling out about what happened to America under the Clinton Administration and people start to see what's beneath all the lies, then they'll say one of the few people who knew before anybody else was Michael Moriarty. And they'll say, "Come back." That's my hope.

The conversation got a little heavy as we debated people in recent history judged by their peers. I brought up Elia Kazan because earlier in the year the famed director received an honorary Academy Award for Lifetime Achievement. Kazan was welcomed by the Academy but not necessarily by the Hollywood community. The division stemmed from Kazan, considered by some to be a turncoat, for naming names during the House Committee on Un-American Activities, leading to the blacklisting of many artists in the Hollywood community. Moriarty countered by bringing up singer/actor Paul Robson who was also a civil rights activist, blacklisted because of his belief in the communist ideology.

When discussing Kazan, Moriarty called him not only a turncoat but a careerist. "That's one of the great diseases of the world, to be a careerist," said Moriarty. "I am not a careerist. If I were I'd still be on *Law & Order*; million dollar a year job. If I sat there I was going to eat what they wanted me to eat. No, no, no, I'm not a little baby you can put up in a highchair."

Moriarty then went on to talk about musicians like Wagner, a noted anti-Semitic whose music was enthusiastically embraced by the Nazi regime. "So many great artists whose politics and soul I hate, Wagner I don't like, the sense of what he did or what he is," said Moriarty. "A lot of musicians who collaborated with the Nazis I loathe, but they're great artists. You cannot deny that. You must live with the fact that God works in mysterious ways and fills these people of bad character with gifts. Go ahead and enjoy it, but know and believe that."

Opening up to the topic of evil, led to the opportunity to talk about a role for which Moriarty earned both an Emmy and a Golden Globe.

PETER: You did an amazing job in the TV series *Holocaust*, speaking of Nazis . . .

MORIARTY: That's where I learned about . . . we talked about careerists, Dorf the character I played was a careerist in Germany. He was not a racist, not politically motivated, he just wanted to get ahead, go up in the system, feed his family, you know? He was the banality of evil. He was this little worker drone who made the system work. He wasn't this raging, hate-filled person. He made the machine work. There's the big danger. Without them Hitler doesn't have a chance. So, I learned about careerists. That's all he was, a careerist and he was part of the most awful machine, one of the most awful machines to ever walk the Earth.

PETER: How do you get into the skin of a character like that when you get the script? What do you do to bring a character like him to life?

MORIARTY: Well, it's an act of faith and that's the most disturbing role I've ever had to play. Because there we were shooting in Vienna, outside Vienna in a real concentration camp called Mauthausen, and I had to sit in an SS uniform with my jackboots on right next to a real oven, and then go shoot the scene inside the showers where they killed people. It was the most disturbing experience because life and art started blurring. You knew it really happened. And the man who was the head of costumes in Vienna had served the Nazis. It got very, very scary.

PETER: How did it affect you as far as your career is concerned? Because even though Hollywood knows it's a business, there are people who have a hard time differentiating between an actor and their character. For instance

I was recently watching a television series where someone was saying they like the actor, Ralph Fiennes, but they can't seem to get pass the fact he played such a heinous character in *Shindler's List*. Did that happen to you with *Holocaust*?

MORIARTY: Oh yes! You know how much money I turned down? I think about $15 million in offers to play bad guys and Nazis. I hung in there. I said, no, no, no! I went into "B" films, schlock films beating up leading men. And I waited and I waited and then *Law & Order* came along and I had a role with some sense of integrity to it. So, my career is quite remarkable compared to, let's say, [John] Malkovich, who's now just playing bad guys; wonderful actor, but trapped in bad guys. Chris Walken, trapped in bad guys and crazy guys. I fought and fought and it cost me a lot of money but I won.

PETER: Yet by the same token you talk to many an actor and they'll say the fun IS playing the bad guy, so maybe Walken and Malkovich are enjoying it.

MORIARTY: I saw a man die because of playing too many bad guys. He was a sensitive artist named J.T. Walsh and he died of a heart attack not long ago.

PETER: About a year ago.

MORIARTY: Yeah, and I know why he died. It was not because of his heart condition or his drinking or his smoking. It was the fact he could not be cast in anything but bad guys. His soul was broken; he was such a sensitive man.

PETER: I guess one of his last roles was in *Sling Blade*.

MORIARTY: I did a film with him, *Crime of the Century* about the Lindbergh kidnapping. If you take a man with that kind of sensitivity and constantly put him in bad guy roles it hurts his soul, he goes home every night with the words of evil and he is a good man, but it hurts him and kills him, he finally gives up.

PETER: And that's what you think happened to J.T.?

MORIARTY: Yes, absolutely, I have no question about it. They fed him evil. He did not become evil and he died so he would no longer have to go to work and play evil.

PETER: Having said that how much of a character do you bring home while you're shooting, be it a good guy like Ben Stone or an evil character?

MORIARTY: Well, being the actor I am I can't play bad guys. I flirt with the idea when I'm low on money and I need a job but I try as much to fight against it because words are like seeds. You are the fertilizer in which they are dropped and the words add up to evil. It's very disturbing inside your heart. You grow very sad and very angry. And in small ways you take it out on your family and your friends, it's not good.

Moriarty was thinking past his acting career to a potential future in Canadian politics. It was his goal to gain Canadian citizenship and then look at a life in public service. He believes the world is in total disarray and he distrusts socialism and what he calls the liberal direction that really runs the world. He says he won't affiliate himself with any party, but instead will create his own.

Going into politics means going under a microscope, so I questioned whether he was prepared to have his life peeled like an onion by the media if he ran for office. "I've already shown up in article in The Globe & Mail," says Moriarty. "Now I am an alcoholic. Everybody knows I drink. I've been four months sober and it's an interesting trip to take. I got into an interview with what I call an idiot from The Globe & Mail, who's a reformed alcoholic who came to save me. He humiliated me in the article, lied about my Mother. This is major mainstream press in Canada, The New York Times of Canada. That guy just took his personal agenda out on me."

Moriarty then proceeded to weigh in on the politics of Canada from coast to coast, the provincial politics of Quebec and even the municipal politics of Montreal, with opinions and an outlook that could be described as radical to people on both sides of the aisle. Whether you agreed with him or not he was certainly someone who enjoyed the process of debate, which in this day and age is somewhat refreshing. But I wanted to end our chat by getting back to what we know him as best, an actor. However, we headed off the rails once again.

PETER: Clearly you look deeper into a role than the average person does when they pick a role. How do you choose the roles you decide to play? Are you looking for a subtle context?

MORIARTY: It depends on the size of my bank account. That's number one. Pay the bills. My Dad raised me with your pride as a man is you're the breadwinner. That's a man's job. I'm old fashioned. My step-mother was Italian. She treated my father like he was a king. You don't see that these days. It's very hard for men to want to live these days, under the new definition of what a man is supposed to be, by the liberal, socialist feminist movement. It's very hard for men.

We never did get to number two in Moriarty's string of consciousness and our time was coming to an end. It was a rambling hour of conversation; an odd recipe of brilliance, deep thought, radical theories, and controversial opinions, one of the more bizarre encounters of my career. We continued down the rabbit hole of political debate for a few more minutes. But then it was time to return him to his hotel, along with his cup, saucer and spoon.

Chapter 20

Burt Ward

Looking back at the portrayal of Robin on the iconic TV series, *Batman* (1966), makes you wonder how different young Dick Grayson would have been if, as a child, he had taken Ritalin. The overly energetic sidekick to the Caped Crusader was enthusiastically brought to life by a then twenty-year-old Burt Ward.

In August 1995, Ward was still very enthusiastic, as he promoted his book, *Boy Wonder: My Life in Tights*. I learned this, as we spent an hour together on the radio (and I also penned an article for Britain's entertainment magazine, *Empire*), where he gleefully shared some of his exploits of being young and running loose in 1960's Hollywood.

Right off the bat, Ward was in character, bellowing "Hello Citizen!" when introduced on the air. He then dove directly into the deep end of the titillating elements contained in his book, when asked why he was sharing the secrets now.

WARD: Well, because only now is the story complete. When I entered *Batman* as a naive twenty-year-old, who had only dated a couple of girls, I met Adam West, who immediately introduced me to the wildest sexual debauchery you can imagine. Within a few months, we were like two hungry sharks in a world of unlimited halibut. Maybe I'm a little too harsh on Adam. Actually, to be more descriptive, he was more like a killer whale in a world of plankton. Together, we had this wild time.

Ward claimed it was only in the last five years that he found what he called "holy maturity." He finally had balance in his life and the right person, so he could reflect more accurately on what some might call a misspent youth, but Ward had no regrets.

WARD: Oh gosh no, how can you? I mean, we're talking about some of the wildest things you can imagine; things that were absolutely kept from the public. In my book, everything I have in there is only the material and the things people would most likely never have found out about. Everything regular and average I left out, because people already know about it.

To hear Ward talk about his exploits was like listening to a high school jock giving his buddies post-date analysis of the prom.

WARD: When you come into the set at 7:30 in the morning, and you come out of make-up, and the first thing you know, the ladies start coming into our dressing rooms at 7:45, we're talking about wild times in the dressing rooms, on the set, between the shots, in the lunch wagon. When we got home at night after fourteen hours on the set, I think we redefined the meaning of the word pleasure pad. And then, of course, doing the personal appearances on the weekend, that's where it really got wild. And I have to be honest with you, we became like sexual vampires. The 1960s was a period of time when everything was free love. People made love to each other. It was a very open life, you know? So, it wasn't as though we were out soliciting or anything. We were the ones being chased.

While the television series was skewered towards youngsters, Ward's book certainly was not. It even contained a disclaimer warning against minors reading it.

WARD: It's only for adults. In fact, I have a full page warning right in the front of the book that says, "No one under the age of 18 should read this book and no one should even turn the pages if they are sexually conservative or erotically deprived.

PETER: Were you concerned about the image you've had all these years from playing Robin the Boy Wonder and whether you're tarnishing it by bringing out a book like this?

WARD: No, I don't think so, and I'll tell you why. I state right on the back cover of the book, "Our characters were antiseptic, but we weren't." If you remember what we did on *Batman*, the scripts were written very funny. We played them very straight. So, for children, they had the hero worship of superheroes, and we never, ever, in any way tarnished that image. For the adults, they remember the nostalgia of the comic books. And for teenagers and college kids, it was that put-on style, you know? We used to say, "We put on our tights to put on the world!" So, I don't think it tarnishes the image at all. On the contrary, what it does say is, "Hey everybody, while you thought this was going on, in addition to that, we were human beings and not just comic book characters, and this was one of the wildest times you could possibly imagine." We found that, just by the way we stood, affected women dramatically, and if you look at our show, you'll see we always stood with our legs open, our fists on hips, and our bat bulges forward, which had a profound effect on women!

PETER: We're hearing about this book and all the things that went on backstage, but there was always been talk about the relationship between Batman and Robin. That must have annoyed you over the years?

BURT: Well, not at all. Let me tell you something. I'll give you the whole story in a nutshell. In the 1950s, there was a psychiatrist, who felt the Batman-Robin relationship represented a wish dream of two homosexuals, and he based it on the fact that Batman was a muscular older man, who took this young teenage boy under his wing, who agreed to everything Bruce Wayne asked him to do. I mean, kids don't normally agree to what parental suggestions are. And in this case, this was not an adoption. It was very clear it was a different kind of relationship, but it didn't necessarily have to be homosexual. Now, I've gotten a lot of questions when I was filming the show.

They say, "Well you know, it's kind of a strange and unnatural relationship." And I'd say, "Hey wait a minute! What's so strange and unnatural about two guys who run around wearing tights and live together?" (Laughter.) I will say this, though, when we did put on our costumes, and you look at the opulence of the Wayne Manor and the impenetrable dark cave and they spend so many long hours together, I mean, I can see where some people might start to think in certain directions. But in our own personal case, we were out fighting all these heinous girls off and sometimes even cheek to cheek as we did it.

Batman was only on the air three seasons, from 1966 to 1968, yet, thanks to two decades of personal appearances well after the show ceased production, Ward continued to cash in on the sexual interest his character had earlier banked for him.

WARD: This is where Adam and I would often do appearances together. I must tell you the life of being a super hero, so to speak, and our show in particular, just drew people to us. They flocked to us and they went crazy! Even in Los Angeles, where we lived, when we would date somebody or go out with them, if we went out with somebody else the next night, we often found women were banging on our windows while we were bedded down with other women!

The subject was still sex, when I asked Ward about the lure of the character on teenagers.

PETER: Do you think part of the draw for the teenagers was that a lot of the boys wanted to be Robin?

WARD: Well, I don't know for teenagers if it was, but I guess when it came to all the gorgeous villains' girlfriends, I'm sure even the adults wanted to be Batman and Robin. In fact, I must tell you something. You know, my book is true. My book is very wild. But you know during the period of *Batman,* there were thousands of Batman and Robin costumes sold, and these weren't just for kids. We're talking about adults that put them on in their private lives with their spouses or girlfriends or boyfriends.

PETER: Well, I had the cape as a kid.

WARD: Holy closeted crime fighter!

PETER: But I know an awakening for me was the first time I saw Yvonne Craig—hello!

WARD: Let me tell you, now, Yvonne Craig is so beautiful. When she came on to the set the first day of the third season, we needed Turkish towels to wipe up all the drool from the crew members.

PETER: Could that costume she wore as Batgirl be any tighter?

WARD: No, and let me tell you something, it was so form-fitting in every place you can imagine that Adam came over to me and he said to me just before the shot in that very deep voice of his, he said, "Burt, let's make a bat sandwich. I said "Adam, oh my God!" He said, "Oh, girls love it." I said, "Adam, don't talk like that." And we got into this position called the Siamese Human Knot, which was on our show, in which Batman, Robin, and Batgirl were all . . . their bodies were intertwined very closely; the theory being if any of us moved an inch, we'd all strangle. And I'll never forget, just before the shot, I felt this unexpected groping. And I thought, *Oh, my gosh! I can't believe it, first Adam West and now Yvonne Craig! Is going to be this wild!* But it turned out she wasn't the one doing it, it was Adam West! I slapped his hand and that's when I nicknamed him "The Groper."

Playing Robin was a physical challenge for the young actor. Ward was usually suspended from something or other. While he had a stuntman, he often did his own.

WARD: I ended up doing most of my own stunts and getting hurt quite a bit. I had never been in an emergency hospital in my life before *Batman.* I was in one the first four days in a row of the first five days of shooting. They had a policy on *Batman* and it was, "If there was ever anything really dangerous, life threatening, always use Burt." And I think the reason was because I was so low-paid, and because it was cheaper for them to use me and pay my salary and the hospital bills than to pay a high priced stuntman.

One example of the situations Ward found himself in involved three large felines.

WARD: I was hung over three Bengal tigers that were supposed to be trying to get at me. Here I was ten feet above them. They can jump twelve to fifteen feet, as I found out later, and the director and the camera man were ten feet higher then me in a steel protective cage, and my head is being hung over these tigers, and the tigers looked and growled. I think, because I wore a costume, that may have saved me from really getting hurt. But then, the director said to the handlers, "Well, can't you make them do something?" The way I was tied down, I didn't notice, but they hung raw meat over my head, and those tigers jumped up in my face, and the director said, "Great, Burt, realistic! Wonderful! Great!" When I found out about the raw meat, I wanted to kill that director, but he was in that protective cage, so I couldn't get to him!

Ward looked back on his days on the show as an ongoing fun party. He enjoyed working with the guest stars who played villains, and bonding with his co-star.

WARD: I had the greatest time of my life! Even working with Adam, who I really adore—okay?—but who absolutely drove me crazy upstaging me, constantly blocking me from the camera, that I was always having to be on my toes. And even when he said his lines, I must tell you, he spoke his lines so slowly, snails could make love while he's doing it. And he did it on purpose, because his theory was, if I speak twice as slowly as I'm supposed to, the camera will be forced to stay on me twice as long.

That's a sly thespian tip learned by a young UCLA acting student, who got the job because he was selling real estate on the weekends.

WARD: I was fortunate enough to sell a house to a producer, who sent me to an agent, who said to me, "Listen, we have so many clients we can't get work for, don't expect to work for a year, and the only reason we're taking you is because this producer sent you to us." But, nevertheless, they finally sent me out, like about two months after meeting them, and *Batman* the series was the first thing I tried out for, and I got it.

Backstage debauchery aside, Ward maintained that the series itself was good, clean fun for the whole family, and he and West could have continued their roles onto the big screen. However, he saw subsequent *Batman* movies as too dark.

WARD: We did a family show. Our show was oriented towards Mom and Dad and the kids, teenagers. Everybody could watch it. The three *Batman* movies that have come out, the studio must feel they need to present this in a much darker, more ominous, more violent, more degrading way, because they didn't want any association with anything uplifting or wholesome or all American apple pie. And that's the answer to it. I don't happen to agree with it. I honestly think Adam and I could have done an incredible job doing the roles. Let me tell you something, this is not against the other actors, like Val Kilmer or Michael Keaton. They're great, too, but Adam West and I *were* Batman and Robin.

Ward had always been faithful to the role that made him famous. As our conversation came to a close, he signed off in character by bellowing four simple words, "To the batmobile, citizen!"

Yvonne Craig. Photo courtesy of YvonneCraig.com.

Chapter 21

Yvonne Craig

Hitting puberty in the late 1960s meant that just when I discovered that girls existed, I was bombarded with women who were poured into skin-tight leather outfits, which was a real awakening for many other young lads, too. The UK gave us Emma Peel in *The Avengers,* and on this side of the pond, a campy little show gave us not one but two shapely women for boys to drool over: the American tv series, *Batman* (1966), brought Catwoman to our screens, and in 1968, followed up with Commissioner Gordon's daughter, who was also Batgirl.

In March 2001, Yvonne Craig, who had donned Batgirl's cape and mask, was promoting her memoir, *From Ballet to the Batcave and Beyond.* It was a book many had previously tried to coax her into writing, because they thought she was funny and had so many stories to tell. Chatting with her on the radio, I experienced what they were talking about. From her first words on the air, she was bubbly, playful, and an excellent storyteller.

Based on the title of her book, I asked if, back in her classically trained ballet days, she ever thought she would end up playing a superhero in a cape. As was the case with all her answers, she had an optimistic outlook on life.

CRAIG: No, I never dreamed I would, and I just loved it! I had been looking for a series, because no matter how much episodic TV I did, and I did a tremendous amount, nobody ever connected a name with a face. They always say, "Oh, that's um, um . . . well you see her all the time. I don't know who she is, but she works a lot." And so, I was really looking for a series to do.

Craig was a seasoned veteran, busy on the big and small screen. She had done two films with Elvis Presley, was famously painted green for the "Whom Gods Destroy" episode of *Star Trek* (1969), plus had guest-starred on a myriad of comedies and dramas, from *The Man From U.N.C.L.E.* (1965), to *My Favorite Martian* (1965), to *The Wild Wild West* (1966), and more. She was extremely busy going from guest-starring spot to guest starring spot. It was almost like the days of the old studio system, when actors were under contract going from soundstage to soundstage, except that Craig was a free-lancer, never under the control of one studio.

CRAIG: I came in at the tail end of live television, thank goodness, because that was a scary prospect. It was the beginning of filmed television. The studio system was almost phased out by the time I got in. I was offered a contract at 20th Century Fox, because I had done a lot of work at Fox, but it was just before they were about to go under, and I kind of saw the writing on the wall, and said to my agent, "I don't want to be at Fox. It doesn't look like they're going to last another year." This was right after [the highly expensive theatrical film] *Cleopatra* (1963). I kind of liked freelancing and I'm glad I did. It was a little dicier in terms of income, but I certainly had more mastery over my own destiny.

Craig had also done four or five pilots in the hope of getting a series, when she got the call to be part of a show that was already an established hit.

CRAIG: I was really excited to be thought of for the role. At the time they were trying to incorporate this female character in it, it was a big hit! I mean, *Batman* was already a success, so it wasn't like we're going to have to shoot this pilot and find out if anybody's interested and all of that. So, I was very happy to join the group.

I could not pass up the chance to share my prepubescent thoughts with Craig on the air.

PETER: Now, just around the time you got to play the role, and I'm sure you hear this from a lot of guys—

CRAIG: —(laughter)—

PETER: —just around the time you started to play the role on *Batman*—

CRAIG: —uh-huh—

PETER: —was just before puberty for me—

CRAIG: —(laughter)—

PETER: —and along comes this girl in a very tight outfit riding a motorcycle.

CRAIG: Right, right! (Laughter.)

PETER: Do you hear these stories a lot?

CRAIG: I hear these stories a lot, and it's funny, because the age of the child goes anywhere from five, when you think, *My word, he peaked early,* to somebody who is twelve years old when it happened, and yeah, I could understand that. When their hormones shot up, I was the first person they saw in a very tight costume, and they decided maybe girls weren't so bad after all! (Laughter!)

PETER: What was it like for you when you first saw the costume? Was it difficult to get into?

CRAIG: Oh no, it was a really comfortable costume. It was made of a stretch fabric and it had a zipper all the way up the back, and so it was easy in and out. It was very comfortable.

While clearly Craig's Batgirl left a lasting impressing on young boys, her character wasn't lost on young girls, either. At the time of her hiring, producers were looking to broaden their audience base to include more over forty males and prepubescent females.

CRAIG: I thought, *Well, I can understand they'll get over forty males, because the costume was spray-on,* but I thought, *I don't think little girls are going to like me. I think they're either going to be in love with Adam and jealous, or interested in Burt Ward and wondering why I'm on the screen taking up time.*

Over the years, Craig learned on the convention circuit that she made a much bigger impression on girls than she thought. She heard repeatedly how Batgirl was the first role model many girls had.

CRAIG: Women say, "I was so thrilled to know girls could kick butt just as well as, or better than, boys." It's a great feeling, and I really like to hear that from women, because we knew why boys watched (laughter), but I wasn't sure we were getting the young female audience, and I guess we did.

I reminded Craig that she was not the first one from the *Batman* series to write about her experiences. I let her know that, six years earlier in 1995, we had Burt Ward on the air, when he was promoting his book, *Boy Wonder: My Life in Tights*, a book Craig had written the Foreword for. Ward's book was a lot racier in tone than most memoirs, which posed a slight problem for her.

CRAIG: The same fellow, [*Batman* writer] Stanley Ralph Ross, who had been trying to encourage me to write, edited Burt's book. It was relentlessly sexual in nature and extremely explicit. So, it was difficult to write the Foreword (laughter) and make it sound at all sensible! And so, Stanley said to me one time after I had written the Foreword, "Did you know all that stuff was going on?" And I said, "No, I had no idea!" And he said, "Well, neither did I!" Now, Stanley was married, and I was dating somebody, but even if I weren't, we were shooting a new segment every three days on that show, so I mean, we were exhausted (laughter). I don't know where they had the energy for all of it, but it *was* the swinging sixties.

Craig didn't doubt the bacchanalian exploits depicted in Ward's book, but she did take exception to one aspect.

CRAIG: I don't know what went on in their dressing rooms, and this very well could have happened there, and I don't know what happened on tour, because this could also happen to them on tour, but I can assure you they were not doing this on the soundstage behind flats as he infers, because we had children on set visiting almost every day. There's just no way it could have been happening on the set itself because there were too many people around.

Eager for her reaction, I played a portion of the Burt Ward interview for Craig, highlighting where Ward described a scene where Batman, Robin, and Batgirl were all tied together (that portion of the conversation is transcribed in the Burt Ward pages of this book). She responded with about five solid seconds of laughter.

CRAIG: Well, that's too funny! I don't ever remember Adam groping him, but who knows?

Craig never felt out of place coming into an established hit show. She was welcomed right away and it didn't have an all-boys club feel to it.

CRAIG: When I look back on it, I'm really amazed at how nice they were to me, because they were introducing a character which was really two characters. I mean, it was Barbara Gordon, who was going to take up screen time, and it was Batgirl, who was going to take up more screen time, and with as many established characters as there were with the alter egos of Batman and Robin, plus Commissioner Gordon and the Chief and Alfred, and then the guest stars, you would have thought they would have resented it simply because it was taking up film time that could easily have been allocated to them—but they didn't at all. Everybody was just really nice. It's probably the happiest set I've ever, ever worked on. It remained that way for the twenty-six episodes I was on. The cast and crew got along very well and they worked well together. And of course, all of the guest stars were just dying to do that show, because it was so far out for it's time and it was so different from anything they would have normally done. I tell you, it was the best experience I ever had in a working situation. It was just terrific.

Craig touched a little bit on her romantic life during her Hollywood days. In the 1960s, she dated actor Vince Edwards, best known as *Ben Casey* on the hit medical drama (1961). She also dated actor Bill Bixby for a period of time.

PETER: Was it difficult in those days to be in the public eye and dating another celebrity? In this day and age, if you're spotted with someone, it's all over *Entertainment Tonight, Access Hollywood,* and all the tabloids.

CRAIG: It is much more invasive these days, and yellow journalism is just at its peak. I'm hoping it's peaked out! No, you could date whomever you wanted. If you went to industry parties covered by the press, then, of course, you were seen with those people, but they didn't invade your privacy or ask you what was going on, or speculate what might be happening. People just had a lot more privacy than they do today. I find almost everybody is inundated with what people are doing and speculating on what they think and why is she with him. I'm one of those people sitting in my living room, and I never thought I would be (laughter) sitting in my living room saying to the television, "Who cares! Who really cares?" There's a lot of tabloid journalism, and I don't really think we're the better for it.

Still, Craig continued sharing her rosy outlook on life even when discussing what had to be a somewhat creepier time for her, when she was briefly under contract to eccentric billionaire, Howard Hughes. She wrote about it in her book in a chapter subtitled "Give Me Back My Guinea Pig!" Hughes saw Craig when she first got to Hollywood and contacted her manager, telling him he was getting back into show business and wanted to put Craig under contract to play the lead in a movie based on a book he had the rights to.

CRAIG: I met the writer, and it all seemed on the up and up, and he had me under an exclusive contract, and it was okay, and then strange things began to happen . . . and then, stranger things began to happen . . . and then, one day, the straw that broke the camel's back was I went home to my apartment and found there was nothing in it. I mean, my clothes were gone, my canned goods were gone, my dog was missing, and my guinea pig was gone! And just before I was ready to call the police, his secretary came in and said, "Oh, I'm so sorry you arrived here before I did." She said, "Mr. Hughes decided this was not a safe place for you to live. So, he has moved you out and all of your belongings to the Chateau Marmont." So, he moved me, and the Chateau Marmont would not accept pets. My dog went to a vet and was boarded there, and my guinea pig went who knew where!

Craig was sequestered away at the hotel for about ten days. At one point, she called down to the front desk, trying to make a phone call out.

CRAIG: The woman downstairs said to me, "I'm sorry but you're not allowed to make a phone call out," and I said, "No, no, I'm sorry, I think you probably mean I'm not allowed to make long distance calls, and that I can understand, but I can certainly make phone calls." And she said, "Why don't you come downstairs?" And so, I went downstairs, and there she sat and she said, "I could lose my job for telling you this, but I think you need to know Mr. Hughes has requested no phone calls go in or out.

PETER: Why?

CRAIG: Who knows? I never saw the man. I never met him. They used to call me up and say, "Mr. Hughes would like to see you." And then, I would go to the office where they said he was going to be, and then I would sit and wait, and sit and wait, and sit and wait, and he never showed up, and then it would get dark, and then they would say, "Well, Mr. Hughes never sees anybody when it gets dark." And then I would go home. And now looking back on it, with the stuff that's come out about him, I have a feeling—and this is so creepy—but I have a feeling he saw me . . . even though I didn't see him.

PETER: That's a movie plot all on its own.

CRAIG: Ew! It's just really . . . urgh! So anyway, when she told me this, I said, "Thank you very much." And I went down to the corner, made a phone call, and picked up a newspaper, and the next day went out and rented another apartment. And I just said to my manager, "Oh look, tell Mr. Hughes when he has a script ready for me to do, I'm happy to read it, but I do not want to be under contract to him and I do not want to be just sitting around waiting for work. And so, when he has it, get back to me."

Howard Hughes never got back to her. This was just a strange first chapter in Craig's arrival to Hollywood in her accidental transition from ballerina to actress.

CRAIG: I was with the Ballet Russe de Monte Carlo back when ice covered the Earth. I was a soloist with the company. We were stationed in New York, and we would tour the United States and parts of Canada. I came out to Los Angeles, because I was getting ready to go with a ballet company in Europe, and came to Los Angeles to study for the summer, and just inadvertently got into the movies.

Acting wasn't on Craig's radar. She wanted to be a ballerina since she was ten, but she soon discovered she enjoyed acting.

CRAIG: I think, at the time I began acting, if somebody had said to me, "You will never dance again," I would have gone home and taken a gun to my temple. If someone had said to me in the beginning, "You will never be allowed to act again," I would have said, "Okay," because it wasn't this burning desire. Now, as I began to do it, I realized I really like it and it was far more interesting because you're using all of you, including voice, as opposed to just technique and your body for dancing.

Craig laughed all the way through our conversation, but the biggest laugh I got out of her was when I asked this question:

Yvonne Craig on the cover of her book *From Ballet to the Batcave and Beyond.* Photo courtesy of YvonneCraig.com.

PETER: Judging by the picture on the cover of your book, one of the things I'm sure ballet was able to teach you for roles like Batgirl is that you can kick a basketball player in the head without leaving the ground.

CRAIG: (Laughter.)

PETER: What else did your ballet training do to help you in your roles?

CRAIG: I'll tell you what it did. I've never known a ballet dancer to ever, ever be late. They are never late. You are disciplined. You are there when the class starts, or you don't get to take it. It's just very good training for discipline, and I think that's a good thing.

PETER: Would you consider yourself at the time to be—because we talk to you now, and you're fun, you're jovial—would you consider yourself a serious person when you were in ballet?

CRAIG: Yes, yes. I think all ballet dancers have that little "I am a little serious rat" look. Because we all pulled our hair back, or at least then we did. We all skinned our hair back and looked very intense. But you are intense. It's interesting with ballet. With ballet in particular, there is only one right way. I mean, there is only one first, second, third, fourth, and fifth position, and if you're not in it, you're wrong! So, you can take comfort in knowing there is definitely a standard, and if you don't meet that standard, you're incorrect. That's the good part about it. It's very wearing on body parts. I danced, but I didn't continue to dance professionally as some of my ex-roommates, and they all are on their second set of hips. I mean, I have the original ones I was born with, but they are all into hip replacements.

PETER: You did get to dance in *In Like Flint* (1967).

CRAIG: When I look back at it, I got to do a lot of dancing, but the ballet dancing I got to do was definitely *In Like Flint*. That was wonderful! I played a Russian ballerina. Unfortunately, it was shot from such a distance that, when you saw the film, it could have been anybody (laughter). I knew it was I, but nobody else would have known except maybe my family, because they knew how I moved. It looked like it was shot on Stage 10 from Stage 12!

Craig not only left ballet behind. With the exception of voicing the animated character of Grandma in the children's show, *Olivia* (2009-2011), she left acting in 1976, putting the bright lights and sound stages in her rear view mirror. She did a tremendous amount of adventure travel, going to Africa six times on safari.

CRAIG: I've also been to the *Galapagos* Islands and broke my foot in a lava tube. I've gone white water rafting in Ecuador, and just doing all kinds of fun things!

She then started her third successful career, this time in real estate. She also thoroughly enjoyed her ballet years and her *Batman* years. Back in 2001, she was clearly still laughing it up in the beyond part of her life, too.

Yvonne Craig. Photo courtesy of YvonneCraig.com.

Julie Newmar. Photo courtesy of Sean Black.

Chapter 22

Julie Newmar

S he's the classic combination of brains and beauty: an IQ score that clocks in at 135 and a form that was literally TV's *My Living Doll* (1964), and later poured into the leather outfit of Catwoman on *Batman* (1966-1967). Actress Julie Newmar oozes sensuality in even just the simplest of phrases.

I first talked to the statuesque beauty in January 2009, and again in August 2011, when she was promoting her how-to book, *The Conscious Catwoman Explains Life on Earth*. The fan in me came out, when I brought up one of her earliest television roles. My mother was a seamstress and had what is known as a seamstress dress form or sewing mannequin. As a six-year-old, I had named the mannequin Rhoda after the robot character Newmar played in *My Living Doll*, the sitcom she starred in with Robert Cummings.

NEWMAR: I was in black and white then. That's your mother's era. It's embarrassing, isn't it?

PETER: Did you find, especially back in the early days of Hollywood, that people didn't take you as seriously as they should?

NEWMAR: No, I think they did. I got to do a lot of really extraordinary things. Even on *My Living Doll*, I got to play the piano, I direct recorded Chopin. They wrote a whole story for me as a ballet dancer, which I was one time in my life, although I'm almost six feet tall and could never join the ballet company, but I got to do it then. No, I think I've fared rather well. I was a pianist, and then a dancer, I think I loved that most. I was an actress. I won the Tony Award on Broadway. [She won the Tony Award for Best Featured Actress in a Play for her role as Katrin Sveg in the 1958 Broadway production of *The Marriage-Go-Round*.] Then, I was a mother. That counts, I think. Most women would agree. Then, my fifth career was in real estate. That's what supports me. And now, I'm writing, because I enjoy it.

Julie shared her thoughts via JulieNewmarWrites.com. It was a blog, sharing stories of things that happen to her and the places she's been. At the time of our conversation, her site told the story of a Playboy holiday gathering.

NEWMAR: The other day on New Year's Eve, I went to Hugh Hefner's New Year's Eve Party, and you'd be amazed. I had a pretty good time. Wait till you get to the part about the naked girls and the white balloons! Of course, there are other things on the site, as well.

The conversation quickly turned to her defining role as Catwoman. Newmar was one of three actresses to play the feline femme fatale on the hit television series. She originated the part that was later taken over by Lee Meriwether and Eartha Kitt, but her portrayal that set the mould.

PETER: How did the part come to you, Julie?

NEWMAR: I think desperation on the producer's part. They make decisions yesterday about what they want to do tomorrow, and then they flew me out from New York, and they gave me the script on Monday. We had a fitting on Tuesday, and I was on the set Wednesday shooting. Things happen that fast.

PETER: Why do you say desperation on their part?

NEWMAR: Because everything's that way in television! You know that (laughter)!

PETER: Did you ever think, when you were doing Catwoman, that it would become such an iconic part?

NEWMAR: No, but it was very popular at the time, and all sorts of very famous people wanted to be on the show. Frank Sinatra tried to talk his way into it. Everybody tried to get into that show, because their kids loved it so much.

PETER: That was a period when *I Dream of Jeannie* (1965) was on and Barbara Eden couldn't show her navel. Were there any concerns with Standards and Practices at the network concerning how tight your cat suit was, for instance, or how you looked?

NEWMAR: Now, now, now, I was fully clothed.

PETER: Oh, I know you were fully clothed, but it was a very form-fitting piece of clothing you were in.

NEWMAR: You have to tell your mother I used to make my own clothes. My grandmother taught me how to sew, and my mother gave me a Singer sewing machine. I used to make my own clothes when I was a teenager. When I got hold of the Catwoman costume, I turned it inside out, put it on the floor and showed the seamstress how to make the seams. And that's why it looked as if it was just liquorice poured over me. So, it helped to know something about making clothes.

Newmar was replaced on *Batman* by Meriwether in a TV movie and Kitt on the series, but she wasn't one to hold a grudge, even praising Kitt for bringing new vitality to the character and the best purr of the actresses to play the role.

PETER: Did it bother you that you were replaced in the role?

NEWMAR: Oh, no! It's good to have competition. I think it's interesting.

PETER: Now you see that's the 135 IQ talking, because I know most people would just be pulling their hair out, with someone taking their part.

NEWMAR: You know, I always felt as if I was underappreciated, but I was not underappreciated. And what I mean by that is, because of my dancing, I had such a distinct dancing background and career. I was at Universal Studios at the age of nineteen. I ran the dance department. I was their choreographer. Can you imagine? That's when they had actors under contract, and they had acting theater classes, and all that kind of thing, but I do think the Catwoman really employed the dancing art, so to speak, or the flexible body being able to speak, or telling with your body as an acting instrument. It was the physicalization. I always think I choreographed the words as Catwoman.

As popular as her roles had been, Newmar also had another unique acting accolade. There's a movie featuring her name in the title, *To Wong Foo, Thanks for Everything! Julie Newmar*. The 1995 comedy tells the story of three New York drag queens, who embark on a road trip. The title refers to an autographed photo of Newmar the trio carries with them on their journey.

Newmar, who had a cameo in the film, didn't find the concept for the movie odd. In fact, she found it flattering.

NEWMAR: It sounded like a good idea, but I did want to read the script. You never know what someone is going to say about you.

PETER: You were really careful about reading the script.

NEWMAR: You read *Entertainment Weekly*. You watch television. You know what they do to people these days.

PETER: Yes, I do.

NEWMAR: Oh, you have to be careful walking down the street and they're photographing you. It happens to politicians.

PETER: That brings up another point. You look at the era of Hollywood you worked in primarily, would you be comfortable with the way the tabloids and the paparazzi work today if you were starting again now?

NEWMAR: Well, you know what I've noticed? The really smart ones, like Angelina Jolie, she just stands there with her mouth quietly closed and her eyes are just softly looking out there. And let me tell you what happens. The paparazzi are out there, in her case, there would be a hundred; in my case maybe ten. They'd be screaming, "Julie, Julie" or "Angelina, Angelina, over here, over here." And they try to trip you up, they try to get you to do awkward or stupid things and you have to be really in control of yourself in these situations these days.

PETER: Everybody is also looking for a feud. A couple of years ago, you had a feud with one of your neighbours.

NEWMAR: Yeah, but it turned out really well. Jim Belushi had me on his show [*According to Jim*, 2001]. He wrote a wonderful show with me as the main character. We had great fun together and we're now good friends.

Newmar and Belushi lived next door to each other for the better part of two decades, and while they say good fences make good neighbours, this was actually a feud started over a fence. Reports stated that Belushi wanted a higher fence for more privacy, but Newmar wanted it lower because a higher fence would rob her prized gardens of much needed sunlight. The battle went on for years with back and forth arguments, verbal volleys, and even an accusation by Belushi of Newmar tearing down his fence and throwing an egg at his house. She complained about noisy air conditioners, among other things. In the end, a $4 million lawsuit was levelled, eventually to be settled in mediation.

PETER: It was splashed all across the magazines and the tabloids. Was the situation blown out of proportion?

NEWMAR: Oh, of course, of course! My gosh, you can't take things seriously even when it's said about you. It's not good to end up in law court, it is not good, because justice is not really, truly played out there. So, these things have to be resolved quietly and without public attention.

She preferred being on the boards. In her very first speaking part on Broadway in *The Marriage-Go-Round* (1958), she snagged a Tony Award. She was also in *Silk Stockings* (1955) and *L'il Abner* (1956) on Broadway.

NEWMAR: I think actors always like the stage more, because they're more in control there. Also, you can do it from start to finish. As we all know, in films, you may shoot the end and then the middle, so there's not that feeling of cohesion and an emotional exchange you have with a real audience. It's awkward to try to be funny in films, because you want to make an audience laugh. You want to get some feedback. But everything is different and has its own joys, and television is wonderful, because you have to do it so fast and spontaneously.

There was nothing but rave reviews when Newmar started her career.

NEWMAR: The writer wanted Bridgette Bardot. Then, they wanted someone Swedish. My grandmother is Swedish. They wanted someone tall to play opposite Charles Boyer, who was about five-feet-eight, and I'm five-eleven. Of course, I had to audition for everybody before I got the part, but it was a charming comedy that closed to standing room only on Broadway. It also had Claudette Colbert. It was a wonderful experience for me.

Newmar was in her early twenties, when she got her Broadway start opposite such seasoned and celebrated pros, but she was never star struck.

NEWMAR: You know, I've never asked anyone for their autograph, anyone who was famous. It's just the work you do. It's your family, and it would make the stars awkward if you behaved as if they were so much greater and wonderful than you. It's kind of off-putting.

While she might not be star struck, many were star struck by her, usually men, and the age range was wide.

PETER: Speaking of awkward, there must be a lot of fifty-year-old guys who come up to you and are just giggling fools when they meet you.

NEWMAR: Fifty! They're seventy, they're thirty. Oh, I have to tell you about a funny thing that happened at a personal appearance. You know, we sign autographs and people come up and meet you. I love these things, by the way, because it's like people all day long just telling you how much they love you and appreciate you. But anyway, this man walks up to me with his son, who's really too young to be there, maybe between three and four. He hid behind his Dad's knees. And the Dad says, "Oh, she's very famous! She's the Catwoman, you know?" So, I give him an autograph and I'm polite and all of that. And then, about a minute later, the grandfather walks up. He walks straight up to me and he's got this real look in his eyes and he says, "Hmmm, I really do like you," almost I would say slightly licentious, you know? It's a very, very wonderful memory of mine.

I managed to have a conversation with Julie without becoming a giggling fool or licentious, and it, too, was a wonderful memory of mine, one of two radio conversations with the acting icon. To paraphrase a certain title, thanks for everything, Julie Newmar.

Chapter 23

Phyllis Diller

Phyllis Diller was a groundbreaking trailblazer and a pioneer for many female comics following in her footsteps. Her stand-up career dominated the last half of the last century. I caught up with Phyllis in September 2004, two years after she retired from the stage. She was promoting a documentary, *Goodnight, We Love You* (2004), that chronicled her last performance in May 2002 in Las Vegas.

Phyllis Diller's trademarks were her biting humour, an over-the-top fashion sense, and a cackling guffaw of a laugh. On the radio, listeners couldn't experience an outfit, but her distinctive laugh hit them right out of the gate, the moment she was introduced on the air.

PETER: Hello Miss Diller. How are you?

DILLER: Well, hello there, Peter Anthony Holder (cackling laughter). What a name!

PETER: Thank you.

DILLER: I looove it!

It wasn't the grind of being on stage that brought her curtain down, but rather the traveling to get there, specifically airports.

DILLER: I had to take a wheelchair in the airport. The airports have gotten so big. I can walk. I walk great, but I can't walk that far, that fast, that long. And anyway, after forty-eight years of that really disciplined business, it was time. I still enjoyed the onstage hour, but all the stuff around it was a lot of work.

PETER: To hear you tell it, you are now leading a sedentary life and don't miss stand-up.

DILLER: Nope, because it was a big, big tense business and it was work. And I'm enjoying being a lazy slob!

Like Fang, the imaginary husband of her routines, nothing could be further from the truth. Diller was busy. She had a recurring role on the daytime soap, *The Bold and the Beautiful* (2003-2012), playing Gladys Pope, and she was an accomplished painter, a talent she only developed in 1986.

DILLER: I've got a whole new life now. That's why it wasn't a big deal to give up the last one. I've got a new one waiting.

On the subject of comedy, I pointed out a difference between her generation of stand-ups and the ones that followed:

PETER: You did stand-up for quite a long time, and it's something I can say your generation of comics continue to do. It seems today a lot of people who get into stand-up comedy get into it as a route to getting a sitcom and then maybe acting in movies and never do stand-up again, but you did it for quite a long time.

DILLER: Well, you realize for Jerry Seinfeld, it's his main love, and he keeps going back to stand-up. And so does Robin Williams, and Robin, of course is a big movie talent. They love stand-up, and I'll tell you why . . . there is no greater thrill!

PETER: You enjoy the adulation of the crowd.

DILLER: The word is not adulation; I never worked for that at all. The laugh!

PETER: Right.

DILLER: Wow! 2,000 people all laughing at once. Oh baby, there's nothing like it!

The beginning of Diller's career saw her as the only female comic with any kind of reputation. She remained the only woman for an entire decade, until Joan Rivers and Totie Fields came along.

PETER: I guess Moms Mabley did some stand-up, as well, back then.

DILLER: Well, I'm not counting her.

PETER: Okay, why wouldn't you count Moms Mabley?

DILLER: I don't know, I think she had no teeth! (Long cackling laughter.)

PETER: What do you think of the female stand-ups around today?

DILLER: Some of them are brilliant, and some of them aren't. Of course, what the hell, that's the way everything is. There's always a few wonderful, wonderful brilliant ones, who will make it to the very top. And there are others, who will make other careers based on what they've done in stand-up, like writing and editing, if they're devoted to comedy. Not everyone has to make it in front of the audience.

Diller doesn't believe the world of stand-up is any tougher for a woman than it is for a man.

DILLER: It has nothing to do with it. You're either funny or you aren't. It is not tougher. Some ladies will tell you it is, because they'll find any excuse to say why they didn't make it.

The Diller stage persona we grew accustomed to was one developed over time. She described her character as "a dummy harridan, who was always just a little this side of chic and always outrageous in some way, the hair, the boots, and always, gloves." She pointed out that all clowns wear gloves, even Mickey Mouse. Every aspect of the Diller character was a creation, except for one thing—the laugh.

DILLER: Well, that's my natural laugh and I love to laugh. It's very healthy to laugh and more people ought to laugh more often!

Diller was certainly a late bloomer. Her painting career began in her seventies, and her stand-up didn't start until she was thirty-seven, which, back then was considered really old in the biz. Diller was a housewife raising five children before she set foot on stage, auditioning at The Purple Onion in San Francisco. Many tried to talk her out of it.

DILLER: They said, "Don't give up your day job," and that was a dear friend.

Being a comic success was a necessity for Diller. She needed to be the breadwinner in her family.

PETER: You managed to keep your family under wraps through your entire career, and maybe this is the difference between how business was done then, without the glare of media, the way it is today. You managed to have a family, raise five kids, and no one ever really knew about it. They just knew the persona of Phyllis Diller on stage.

DILLER: Well, that's true. That is true. It was just one of those things. I simply had to do it, because I married to a man who could not make a living, so, thank God, or I never would have been me. If I married a man who could support the family, I would just be the funniest woman on my block.

PETER: You became a comedian out of necessity, I mean, a love for the business obviously, but out of necessity.

DILLER: That is true. And there's nothing like poverty to inspire you.

Fang, her spousal creation, bore no resemblance to her own husband. It was all part of her imagination, and the name came to her spontaneously on stage.

DILLER: It was an ad-lib very early in my business. It was the first character I ever invented. In other words, I was simply talking about every husband. I remember the bit was I had a car accident. I had to call home and tell old Fang face. In those days, most families only had one car and it was really the man's car and it was a part of him. So, it was a terrible thing to have to call home and tell him you've wrecked it. And I said I had a little accident at the corner of Post and Gary. And he said, "Post and Gary don't cross." I said, "They do now!"

Although the bulk of her career was stand-up, Diller wasn't unfamiliar on the big screen. She had over thirty movie credits to her name, but while she enjoyed the films, the process for her was less than thrilling.

DILLER: I enjoy the stand-up most of all, because it's instant gratification. You hear those laughs and you feel wonderful after the show. Making movies is a very boring process. God, I admire movie stars so much for their patience.

Those who came in contact with Phyllis Diller when she wasn't on stage were surprised by the normalcy of her own appearance. Many thought they would see her in character all the time.

DILLER: Limo drivers would come to the airport thinking they would recognize me, and they wouldn't hold up a sign with my name on it. They'd look at everybody and they couldn't find anybody they thought was I, because I don't look like the harridan on stage.

Diller's face also changed through the years. While it was taboo back then to openly discuss having work done, Diller was always forthcoming about plastic surgery. She first went under the knife in 1971 at age fifty-five.

DILLER: God, it's made a new woman out of me! I had eye bags and a chin droop. So, I went in for everything. My nose was a mess. They named a movie after my old nose . . . Z! So, they did a complete face job, eye job, neck job, everything job. Boy, I came out looking like a million!

PETER: You talked about the work you had done and this was unheard of at the time.

DILLER: Not at the time, it was brand new, no one ever did that. That's because I'm that kind of a person, you see. I'm a completely open person. If you want to be friendly with people, you have to be open. You have to be honest. I have sat with women, in the past, who have asked me a bunch of questions about plastic surgery, who obviously had already had it. They were faking the whole conversation, or probably thinking I was fooled!

Diller often worked with Bob Hope, even traveling to war zones to entertain the troops. She described the military transport flights as "flying in a basement," seated in a plane with no windows and very few amenities. Entertainment-starved GIs at the fronts were some of the best audiences, even for someone who looked like Phyllis Diller.

PETER: You travel with Bob Hope and there's always a Raquel Welch, or an Ann Margaret, or some beautiful young girl out there to entertain the troops, and out walks the persona that is Phyllis Diller.

DILLER: Oh that's right. I was the ugly one, you know. And it was fun. He'd [Hope] stand me next to a great looking brunette like Raquel Welch and ask, "Is it true blondes have more fun?" And of course, it isn't in that case. He always made fun of me, and I loved that!

Diller and Hope were close friends, and she acknowledged his helping hand.

DILLER: He hired me for so many things, television and the movies, and it was a big part of my career.

Diller wrote almost all of her material, carving out a unique style all her own.

DILLER: I structured it all and wrote, I would say, seventy-five percent. The others, were just one-liners I bought here and there.

She acknowledged that success in comedy was hard work.

DILLER: It's a very difficult thing. It's a long way from the living room—when you're funny at parties—to the white-hot lights and a large room with thousands of people.

Difficult as it may be, for almost half a century, Phyllis Diller's immense talent made it look easy.

Chapter 24

Shirley Eaton, Bond's Painted Girl

Death has never looked so beautiful. In the 1964 James Bond film, *Goldfinger*, actress Shirley Eaton played Jill Masterson, who met her demise by being suffocated in gold body paint. It was an image that catapulted her to international fame, an image forever locked in the mind of Bond fans.

In September 2000, I talked to the early Bond girl. She was promoting a calendar and book she was part of, called *Swingin' Chicks Of The 60s* [May 2003, by Chris Strodder]. Eaton was amazed that, all these years later, people still recognized her on the streets, and she was shocked that she was still considered a pin-up. I wanted to know if she ever got tired being asked about her iconic role, since more than thirty years had passed. The painting process for the famous scene was a long one, but it didn't bother Eaton.

EATON: No, not really, I'll tell you why. I made twenty-nine films. I made twenty-one before *Goldfinger*, but it was *Goldfinger* that made me internationally known. So, you can hardly be angry at that, can you? (Laugh.) Actually, it was not so bad being painted, because I was painted with a wonderfully soft brush, but it was getting it off that was the bother. That took ages just with a sponge and soap and God knows what. And it was also very uncomfortable, very hot. But, I'm glad I did it!

There are stories of other actors, who had been painted for roles with dire consequences, some who had life-threatening allergic reactions to the paint. [See the Buddy Ebsen chapter.] That was never a concern for Eaton on the Bond set.

EATON: Well, it can suffocate you. So, there was an area left of the front of my tummy from my rib cage to my bellybutton that was left unpainted, because the shot was on my tummy, so it didn't matter. And also, the director, Guy Hamilton was wonderful. He shot the scene from two different angles and he shot it much quicker than we normally do, so I didn't get too hot.

PETER: As I mentioned off the top, you still seemed surprised that people recognize you.

EATON: Yes, well it's wonderful, isn't it? It was thirty-six years ago. I don't know how long you want me to chat on here because I'm quite a chatterbox.

PETER: Oh, take as much time as you want!

EATON: I worked from the age of twelve. In the theater, I was a singer and dancer, and then my first film was with Dirk Bogarde, a cameo, three scenes with him, when I was sixteen (*Doctor in the House*, 1954.) [Shirley had also appeared in the television series, *For the Children* (1950) and *Parent-Craft* (1951) previously, as well as several unaccredited movie appearances.] Then, I never stopped making films from then on from sixteen to thirty-two. I married at twenty, had my first son at twenty-two, my second son at twenty-nine. And I only made two films after my second son was born, because I just couldn't do what all the wonderful women out there try to do—it's juggle lives. You come to a crossroads. I think every woman does at a certain stage, so I gave it up.

Eaton stayed out of the limelight for a long period, happily raising her family. However, in 1994, she became a widow. After grieving for what she called "two horrendous years," the mother of two and grandmother of four needed a goal. She started writing her autobiography, *Golden Girl*. The release of her book and doing publicity for it put Eaton back in the spotlight, with appearances on talk shows.

EATON: I'm in the limelight in a different way. I mean, I'm still, so they say, a gorgeous lady. I'm a very lucky lady. I've got good genes. I still look young, although I'm not like I was back in *Goldfinger*. I'm still slim, blonde, and everything. I've got a new life again.

Eaton was surprised by the response upon her return into the public eye. She thought for sure the years away to raise her family would have left her pretty much forgotten.

EATON: Often, when you start very young, you take everything for granted, not in a bad way, in a good way really, and so, I never knew I'd get the feedback I'd get. The moment into the television studios or radio stations or the press now, I get feedback from all the hard work I did years ago, which is rather satisfying, actually!

PETER: What do your kids think—your two sons and your grandchildren—of your sudden resurgence of fame?

EATON: Oh, they're lovely. Well, the grandchildren are very young. They're too young to know Grandma's special. I mean, I'm special to them, but they're too young for all that stuff. Soon, I'll be able to show them some. In fact, my oldest little one is six. She's actually seen me on television. She rang me up and said, "Nanny, I saw you on the television!" It was in an old film. That's the other thing, of course. Over all these years, another reason I haven't been forgotten is because of television and videos and everything, because the old films come back and back and are forever showing.

Her body of work before becoming that Bond body was impressive, especially among British film fans. Eaton starred in many *Carry On* films [*Carry On Sergeant* (1958), *Carry on Nurse* (1959), and *Carry On Constable*

(1960)], and several of *The Doctor* films with Dirk Bogarde. Plus, guest appearances with future Bond, Roger Moore, on his classic TV series, *The Saint* (1962-1968).

EATON: My career was very kind to me in the sense I was in historic type things that don't really die, and also good things.

There were occasions when I talked to a pinup that the shy pubescent kid came out of me, even during an interview.

PETER: To be honest . . . .

EATON: Yes?

PETER: I think the image of you in paint—every teenage boy who's seen that for the first time—it's like, "Wow!"

EATON: Yeeesss! (Laughter.) I know, [current Bond] Pierce Brosnan said he fell in love with me when he was twelve.

PETER: Exactly!

EATON: I've met him several times. He's actually gorgeous. I mean, not just gorgeous, he's a lovely person. And he said just what you said. Isn't that sweet? If you really want me to talk on that level, it's really rather sweet. Everywhere I go, I get men, actors, all sorts of people, at all different ages, by the way, saying, "Oh my God, I had you all over my bedroom wall. I fell in love with you when I was eighteen. I fell in love with you when I was forty." And I get all this wonderful feedback. It's just, you know, wonderful!

PETER: That role you played was a very sexy, very sensual character, and it was done, dare I say, very tastefully.

EATON: Oh, I love you to say that!

PETER: Do you think it would be done the same tasteful way if it were done today?

EATON: No, it's too much. In no way am I a prude. I'm a very liberal, sensual woman, and still am, but there's no mystery left anymore. Everybody is bonking all over the screen. Really, part of sexuality is mystery, isn't it?

PETER: Right.

EATON: It's sweet, what you just said, but people have said that to me before. All you saw when Sean [Connery] and I had that love scene were my legs. I mean, I had the great big pyjama jacket on, didn't I?

PETER: Right

EATON: And people think it was very sexy because it was playful, sensual, and not over exposed. I wonder where it's all going. I don't think we can go much further than we've already gone right now. I'm really not being a prude. It's because I'm a sensual person and think that part of life is important. I'm quite angry about it. It's not from a prudish point of view, it's from thinking things are special. And they're not special anymore, in a way, when they're in your face.

While times have changed to a more politically correct world, some women took umbrage to the term "Bond Girl" and what they perceived it to represent. Eaton, however, had a different take.

EATON: The reason the Bond films are still popular is they're well-made, they're quite moral, and the women have become less subservient over the years. But I hope they don't lose it entirely because they're feel good factor-type films. You come out thinking, *I've seen something that's made me laugh, made me feel a bit sad and excited and there's no big deal.* They're well-made, old fashioned entertainment. And I think that goes with the women, as well. I really do get rather cross with feminists, because I think a real woman knows she's feminine and doesn't have to sort of shout and rant and rave. She knows she holds everything in her hand anyway.

PETER: I think the women in our audience would be upset if I didn't ask the question, which I'm sure you've heard time and time again . . . .

EATON: Oh, I know what you're going to say. Should I tell you want you're going to say?

PETER: Yes.

EATON: What was it like working with Sean Connery?

PETER: Yes!

EATON: Wonderful! Wonderful! A very quiet man in those days, he was only about thirty-two, something like that. He was very attractive, and both of us had chemistry, individually and together. We had it together in the film, which made it sort of magical. Girls out there, he was just gorgeous! I also think Pierce is gorgeous in another way. You know, he's more of a 1990s Bond, isn't he? I mean he's got that little finesse, he's a little more politically correct, finer, and certainly "twinkly," and certainly got this thing you must have, this special quality. But no, for these girls out there, Sean was gorgeous and very attractive, but very professional and no nonsense about him.

When Eaton talked, there was such a positive tone in her voice. I brought that point up to her.

PETER: I hear a certain amount of joy in your voice. It sounds like you just seem to enjoy the whole experience. I've had the opportunity to talk with several actors and actresses over the years, and there's a bittersweet sound to it in some cases, but you seem to enjoy all your experiences and enjoy life in general. Would that be correct?

EATON: Oh Peter, you are reading me rather well, aren't you? That's what I try to do, you know: go shopping, you smile. Don't you?

PETER: Right.

EATON: A smile is free. And you know, usually somebody smiles back. It's that philosophy isn't it? Mind you, I have my blue days, my irritable days, but on the whole I do try . . . oh, isn't that sweet! You've picked it up so well (laughter). I can't tell you more because it sounds like I'm complimenting myself!

Shirley Eaton was a woman whose life was blessed with joy and fulfillment; an extremely successful career that she put on the backburner to raise her family, followed thirty years later by an unexpected resurgence due to her autobiography, then by being part of another book heralding the women of the 1960s, and a companion calendar she graced the cover of. She was also grateful that her place in history was secure because of 007.

EATON: I'm so glad I did it, because I've gone down in cinema history. If the people are talking about Bond films, even people who aren't Bond fanatics, everybody has their favorite Bond woman, it's absolutely true. But you say "the woman who died painted in gold" and immediately I'm thought of, so I'm really pleased.

Chapter 25

Thurl Ravenscroft

The name Thurl Ravenscroft was neither conventional nor recognizable, but the man with the unusual name had one of the most distinctive and durable voices in the entertainment world. It was he who bellowed the signature phrase of Tony the Tiger in Kellogg's Frosted Flakes commercials for more than fifty years. He was also the singing voice in what became a classic children's animated holiday special, *How The Grinch Stole Christmas* (1966).

In February 1999, Ravenscroft joined me on the air for a conversation just days after his eighty-fifth birthday, his voice as strong and deep as ever. When I asked him at the start how he was, right on cue he let loose with a booming, "I'm Grrrr-eat!" There were fewer voices deeper than Ravenscroft's, and I was curious to know where it came from.

PETER: I've got to ask you—this voice of yours, this most recognizable, most deep voice—at what age—tell me you didn't have this voice when you were nine?

RAVENSCROFT: (Laughter.) Oh, no! In fact, when I was a junior in high school, I was a tenor. But when it dropped, it *really* dropped. And my senior year in high school, I sang bass in the choir, and the year before, I was the tenor lead.

PETER: We should mention right off the bat that you started out as a singer.

RAVENSCROFT: Oh yes, for most of my career I was a singer. I didn't do a lot of narration. I did some storytelling for Disney, and I did a lot of singing for Disney. But it wasn't until my late years that I began to do an awful lot of narration.

Ravenscroft's narration work grew slowly over time. One of his earliest gigs was as the voice for The Pageant of the Masters in Laguna Beach, California, an internationally famous art show.

However, it was as a singer that his career saw the most life. Even Tony the Tiger started out as a singing gig for the first few months that Ravenscroft supplied the voice in the early 1950s.

RAVENSCROFT: Maybe for about forty years, I was primarily a singer. I was with Norman Luboff [founder & conductor of the Norman Luboff Choir] and Pete King [Pete King Chorale] Johnny Mann [Johnny Mann Singers] and all the records and things in Hollywood. In fact, back in 1937, I organized the quartet, The Sportsmen, which became famous on all the radio shows. We were the quartet that drove Jack Benny crazy.

His quartet saw a lot of work besides *The Jack Benny Show* (1960). They also supplied harmonies for many of the *Looney Tunes* and *Merry Melodies* cartoons at Warner Bros., but his busy musical work came to an end because of World War II.

RAVENSCROFT: When the war came along, I was the youngest [of the group] and not married, so I went into the Air Transport Command in Washington, DC, flying special missions over the North and South Atlantic.

Those flights saw him carry some pretty important human cargo during World War II.

RAVENSCROFT: One trip, I flew Winston Churchill. We flew George Marshall when he was Chief of Staff. We flew him to Gibraltar and rendezvoused with Churchill there. And the next day, Churchill came on our plane, and Marshall went on Churchill's plane, and we flew down the heart of the Mediterranean to Algiers with an umbrella of Spitfires and P-38s. That's the conference where they decided whether to invade through Italy or through France. And, of course, everybody knows they invaded through France.

After the war, Ravenscroft had to start his career over again. In 1947, he organized a new quartet called The Mellomen, who soon became very busy.

RAVENSCROFT: We were with Edgar Bergen & Charlie McCarthy, and we started doing a lot of things with Disney. I was one of the singing mice in *Cinderella* (1950).

Singing as a rodent was the beginning of a long relationship at Disney. Ravenscroft was part of practically every animated film that came out of the studio. His voice also carried over to the theme parks, first with Disneyland then Disneyworld, where he can be heard on many of the rides.

Ravenscroft's connection with Kellogg didn't start with Frosted Flakes, but rather with Corn Flakes. His quartet had done an on-camera series for Leo Burnett Agency for Corn Flakes, so both the agency and Kellogg were familiar with him and what he could do.

RAVENSCROFT: When they came out with the new character and the new product, somebody said, "Hey, why don't we see what Thurl will do with this." So, they sent a sample script, a character description, and a drawing of Tony. In the script, it asked, "Well Tony, are Frosted Flakes any good?" And Tony said, "Good, they're great!" And I said, "Well, we have to do something with the word 'great.' We've got to make it explode; we've got to make it hit the screen." So, I messed around with a few things and finally I came up with the "Grrrr-eat!" And forty-seven years later, I'm still doing him!

What was remarkable in talking to Ravenscroft was that, at eighty-five years old, his voice hadn't lost any of the timber or clarity it possessed in his youth, and Tony the Tiger didn't sound a day older than he did five decades earlier. Yet, Ravenscroft said that he didn't do anything special to protect or exercise his vocal cords.

RAVENSCROFT: The good Lord's been good to me. My legs are shot, but my voice isn't, so I've been very lucky!

As Ravenscroft put it, he didn't "job" anymore, living a semi-retired life.

RAVENSCROFT: Once in a while, Disney calls me back to do something if they change the dialogue or something, but I still do Tony. In fact, they send a limo for me, bless their hearts. They're wonderful people, the Leo Burnett Agency, as well as Kellogg.

PETER: With all the years you've done these voices, especially Tony the Tiger, and your voice is so recognizable, you must have had interesting situations where you're in a restaurant or a bank or a supermarket and people recognize who you are.

RAVENSCROFT: Yeah, when they hear me talk they say, "I know your voice. Where have I heard your voice?" And all I have to say is, "Does the word 'Grrrr-eat!' mean anything to you?" And immediately, of course, "I know, you're Tony the Tiger!" It's wonderful.

PETER: Now, whose eyes light up the most when they meet you, is it the kid who sees the commercials and recognizes your voice, or someone who's an adult and grew up with Tony the Tiger or The Grinch?

RAVENSCROFT: Both, both! And of course, after Christmas, when The Grinch is on again, that's when people start to say, "Now wait a minute, where have I heard that voice?"

When we spoke, over thirty years had gone by since the production of *How The Grinch Stole Christmas*. Ravenscroft was surprised at the staying power the perennial special had.

RAVENSCROFT: The day we did The Grinch, Ted Geisel [Dr. Seuss] was there, and Chuck Jones the animator, and we thought it would be a one shot. We thought it would be that Christmas and that would be it. We never dreamed thirty years later it would be bigger than ever. It's really something!

PETER: After all these years of being the voice of Tony the Tiger, you probably know it better than anyone else. I'm sure there are people who have worked on the campaign who have come and gone over the years. Do they now defer to you? Do you look at the script and say, "Oh, Tony would never say this."

RAVENSCROFT: Yeah! And some of the young kids coming along, they're anxious to make their name, so they say, "Why don't you do it this way? Now do it that way. Now try this!" And I finally, sometimes, have to say, "May I show you how Tony would do this?" "Oh yeah, please do!" So, I would do it as I *know* Tony would do it. And they say, "That's a wrap! That's wonderful!" All the old hands, of course, all they do is hand me the script and say, "Go!"

PETER: Was there ever a lull over the decades you've been doing Tony, or has it just kept going from the time you started?

RAVENSCROFT: He's kept going from the time we started. There's never been a dull moment. Sometimes, you make more commercials than others, but there's never been a lull. He's always been on and he's always selling. They've changed his character a few times. When I first started Tony, he was a big braggadocio loud mouth, who knew everything about everything, but always got his face pushed in the mud. And then, they decided Tony was going to be different, so they eased it into where he was a warm, friendly, jovial guy, who always helped kids and encouraged them, and that's pretty much what we're doing now.

Ravenscroft was surprised that even in semi-retirement he was kept busy by answering fan mail. A couple of fans put up a website called All Things Thurl, which has led to getting letters from all around the world. Just on the day we spoke, he was prepping over a hundred autographed pictures to send out.

RAVENSCROFT: When you do something that people appreciate and they let you know about it, it's very heart warming. It makes it all worthwhile. I get some letters from people who are sixteen, seventeen, and I get letters from people who are fifty and sixty years old. And they remember growing up with Tony. Oh it's better than applause or anything else. It's really heartwarming.

Ravenscroft had a long and illustrious career, but there was still one thing he didn't get the chance to do.

RAVENSCROFT: I would have liked to record the entire Bible. I was very close to it, but a big name actor beat me out, but I really wanted to do the entire Bible on tape. That would have been the fitting climax for me.

Ravenscroft had turned to religion in his work. On records, he supplied the voices of Jesus and God on many occasions. In those instances, the scripts were more than just words. It added a little excitement for him in the studio.

RAVENSCROFT: It's always a great thrill to be able to do, and make it come alive. The Lord has blessed me with a different voice and a good voice, and when I use it for Him, it's wonderful! I love it!"

His God-given voice was indeed amazing. I would have said "Grrrr-eat!" but, like most people, I couldn't give that word the gravitas that Thurl Ravenscroft did.

Carol Channing. Photo courtesy of Harlan Boll

Chapter 26

Carol Channing

The cliché "living legend" gets thrown around often, but it definitely applied to a woman who was a giant on stage. Tony winner Carol Channing was already in her eighties, when I had my first chance to talk to her in January 2002.

The opportunity arose because Channing was about to release her story in book form, entitled *Just Lucky I Guess: A Memoir of Sorts*. Her publicist, Harlan Boll, had offered up many of his clients through the years. Harlan and several other Hollywood publicists I'd worked closely with knew my reputation of being the kind of interviewer who would ask solid questions, but not ask anything just for the sheer delight in making someone squirm, or probe too deeply into their private life. As I've mentioned, guests on the air were like dinner guests at my home. You want to make them feel warm and welcomed.

Harlan's concern was that Channing had stepped away from the spotlight for a number of years and she hadn't done an interview in almost five. Added to the mix were tabloid stories questioning the life she led with her late husband. Harlan wanted a knowledgeable, fan-friendly, respectful interviewer, who would guide his client as she dipped her big toe back into the sea of media scrutiny. Her book wasn't coming out for another ten months, but

I agreed to interview Channing if Harlan would let me talk to her a second time once the book was released.

Complicating matters was Channing's health. While rehearsing for a show honoring Broadway composer and lyricist, Jerry Herman, she fell down a flight of stairs on a dimly lit stage. The result of the winding staircase tumble was three broken ribs, a chipped elbow, a hairline fracture of a thumb, and seven stitches in her forehead, yet she was a Broadway trooper, who believes the axiom "the show must go on." She was back the next night belting out tunes in honor of Herman. Channing still got an adrenaline rush and a little stage fright before the curtain opened.

CHANNING: I'll tell you what's great is most actors don't feel anything once they're on stage, so I couldn't wait to get back on. Sheer panic will cause you to do anything. You can do the most wonderful things out of sheer panic.

PETER: When you were performing on stage, you do something like *Hello Dolly* (1964) for years and years and years. How do you keep it fresh?

CHANNING: No problem whatsoever. As I say, it's sheer panic before every audience. I mean, people say, "Oh, how are you Carol? How's your son?" And I'd think, *What a heck of a time to ask me. We've got to go on stage in a few minutes!* And I'd just say, "Look, I can't answer you, you know?" This could be the audience that you don't communicate with, but I don't remember anywhere we really didn't. We always say after the show when they're good, "Lock all the doors and windows and don't let them out!"

PETER: I saw a quote sometime ago where you said, "I've been prostituting myself since the fourth grade."

CHANNING: Yes! Well, the reason is, you see I have a book coming out. I wrote a book, can you believe it? I was thinking, *What should I call this?* and I remember the old, old joke of the client to the prostitute, "What's a nice girl like you doing in a place like this?" And the prostitute says, "Just lucky, I guess!" But it's interesting when you do it on stage. I've been prostituting myself since the fourth grade. I wanted to win the school election so I could read the minutes to the school every Friday. And nobody much cared if they were accurate or not as long as they were entertaining. Isn't that marvellous training?

PETER: You had the acting bug from a very early age?

CHANNING: Seven!

PETER: There was no doubt that this was what you were going to do?

CHANNING: No doubt!

PETER: How did your parents feel, when you said you wanted to go into acting?

CHANNING: I told both my parents, and my father said, "You know those are the happier people. Not the people who get out of work, but the ones who find their work." And I never got off the track. I never tried to do anything else.

Great stage performers are used to memorizing their lines, then hitting the boards from overture to curtain call. I asked Channing, who had also appeared on the big screen, what it was like to live in the hurry-up-and-wait world of making a motion picture. She reminisced about the fun she had with her co-stars while appearing in *Thoroughly Modern Millie* (1967), a role that earned her an Oscar nomination in the Best Supporting Actress category.

CHANNING: Oh, yes, I got to talk to Julie Andrews and that was heaven! And I got to talk to Mary Tyler Moore, and we all became awfully good friends.

The title role of Dolly Levi in the 1969 movie eluded her. Although *Hello Dolly* was her signature character on stage, earning her a Best Actress in a

Musical Tony Award, she was passed over for the movie version in favor of Barbra Streisand, which was a disappointment.

CHANNING: Oh certainly, oh yes! I thought the movie was terrible! Naturally I would [have wanted the role]; no we were good friends, Barbra Streisand and I, and all of a sudden I got on my high horse and got mad.

While she reigned on the Broadway stage, in the beginning it wasn't easy. Channing believed the key was to have faith in herself and her talent.

CHANNING: When people ask me, "Do you think I'm good enough to be on Broadway?" I keep thinking, *If you could ask that question, then you'll never make it.* You just have to keep going after it and after it and being fired, and being ignored, and being told you're too tall, or your voice is too low, or some darn thing. But if you just keep at it beyond all sanity and beyond all health, I don't know, something has to be driving you.

Channing has never done a show on stage that was written for her. Every part she made famous was originally destined for someone else, yet to her, that was what she thrived on.

CHANNING: That's an actor's job. The thrill for me of being on the stage is to get into this character if I'm crazy about her. If you love the character enough, it descends on you, and you've got her voice, you've got the way she walks, the way she talks, the way she sings and dances, and the way she thinks, and you get into her, and people who want to be actors, that's their excitement in life.

We had an exchange on discussing what the audience wanted.

PETER: When people go to a Broadway show, do they want to see Carol Channing absorbed by a character onstage or do they want to see Carol Channing?

CHANNING: I'm unaware of the fact there is a Carol Channing. And I bet if anybody asked you, "Now, who are you Peter Anthony Holder?" you would describe somebody you kind of wish you were, or something else. And your friends would say, "Oh for heaven's sake, that's not you!" If you do honest work artistically in any of the Arts, you recreate yourself and don't know it. There's your answer.

It was almost eleven months later in late November 2002 when I got another chance to have an even longer conversation with Carol Channing upon the release of her book, *Just Lucky I Guess: A Memoir of Sorts.* She went deeper with the prostitution analogy from our previous chat in talking about the book.

CHANNING: I realized I was baring my soul. I was an only child, and I was baring my soul to every student in the school. You've got to hand it to them honestly and trust them, and if they don't trust you, you don't get any laughs. And doggone it, suddenly I wasn't an only child. We're all alike. We laugh and we cry at the same things, we have the same emotions, and I've never felt like an only child since. The only thing is it is a form of prostitution. And that is you make love to the audience in your own way, which for me was as a comedienne. Of course, off stage, it's no rotten good for me, because I trusted everyone. I don't know who's an axe murderer and who isn't, and most people can judge that. I can't. From the time I was too little to know, I was up there in school, and you know, it makes a strange person. I mean, it makes you devoid of criticism."

With all she had done onstage, I was curious to know who her favorite collaborator might have been. I was surprised by her answer.

CHANNING: George Burns. Oh, I thought the world of him. Gracie [Allen] chose me and that's like being knighted in St. James' Court. It's a blessing on my head for the rest of my life. Gracie's doctors said she couldn't work, so for the last two years of Gracie's life, George and I worked together, and then we worked after that. We played theaters two more years, and I learned so much I can't tell you. He was like a magnet to work with. He was so happy if I got the laugh. And I said, "George, you're the most generous person I've ever worked with." He said, "You forget, Carol, I wrote the lines."

As with her previous appearance with me on the radio, Channing once again shared another story to best demonstrates her drive, stamina, and love for the stage, despite personal health issues. This time, she regaled the audience with the story of how she battled cancer while working on tour. Channing always thought being on stage was therapeutic for her.

CHANNING: My goal [on stage] is to lift people's lives, and in the process of giving like that, it's healing. At the end of each show, I either felt a lot better or was cured.

Channing was traveling with the show, but then returning to New York on weekends for treatment at The Sloan-Kettering Cancer Center, keeping her illness a secret.

CHANNING: I never told anybody—because the audience—who wants to buy a ticket for somebody who's sick? And I wasn't sick, not as long as I was working. If you can find work you'd do if you weren't getting paid for it, if everybody could find that work, and then throw themselves into it, it's a funny thing how healing it is.

Since she had written a memoir, sharing her life story, I felt I had to ask the questions about her late husband, Charles Lowe. Stories had been swirling around in the press. In May 1998, Channing sued Lowe for divorce in Los Angeles County Superior Court. She accused him of squandering her fortune, abusing her mentally and physically, and having sex with her only once or twice in their forty-two-year marriage. I was compelled to do it as delicately as possible.

PETER: You decided to go away and sit down for four years to write this book, practically in seclusion, and it was during that time period where your name came up in the news again.

CHANNING: Oh it did?

PETER: Yes, I believe you were also on Larry King at one point talking about this very issue. You went through a divorce, or you were beginning to go through a divorce.

CHANNING: I never got it. He died you know.

PETER: Yes.

CHANNING: And I just feel I don't like talking about people who can't answer back. We all have good and bad in us. I know I do. And everybody has good and bad. It's just a question of how well do we handle it. And I just don't want to talk against him.

PETER: I will say one thing, though, because you did make some statements at the time, your husband was also your manager, correct?

CHANNING: Yes, that's right.

PETER: And from some of the statements you made, you said he was somewhat controlling. I just found that interesting, because there were a lot of women like yourself—Doris Day comes to mind—there were a lot of women like yourself who had managers they were married to. The women were the stars, and we found out later that the men were somewhat controlling. Would you say the situation you were in was not unique? There were many people like yourself who were in that situation?

CHANNING: It's not unique, no. You see, it takes such concentration. Every business takes concentration. But in the theater, all you have to do is lose your concentration. It's like walking a tightrope, lose it for a second and think, *Gee, I'm hungry. I wonder what I'm gonna have for dinner,* and, dog- gone it, they don't laugh at that line, they didn't hear it. Or they don't cry at that line, or they're not touched by it, because it takes total concentration from the time that curtain goes up, never to waver. The moment you waver, the audience wavers, and they don't hear what you're saying. And it's eight shows a week, and it's press in between, and all that, and you've got to have a very strong constitution to be in the live theater. But in the meantime, I haven't got time to take care of my personal life or my bank account or any- thing. It happens to many, many people in theater.

I figured at this point that Carol had answered as completely as she was going to. I got the inference that her money was squandered, and as for the sexual part of her marriage, that really wasn't any of my business. If she wasn't going there, I wasn't going to push it. I went back to talking about the craft of acting and the people who inhabit it.

PETER: Do you think that actors by nature are insecure?

CHANNING: Yes, and we have a right to feel that way, because they do take pot shots at us, and they feel it's easy or something. I don't know an actor who doesn't have stage fright before the show. This could be the audience who doesn't get it. This could be the audience we can't reach. You know, there are audiences like that. Benefit audiences are like that. It's mostly inherited wealth and they don't understand the give and take in life.

Carol Channing definitely understood the give and take in life. Her long, illustrious career proved that her audiences got it. In hindsight, there wasn't anything for her to be afraid of.

Mr. Blackwell. Photo courtesy of The House of Blackwell.

Chapter 27

Mr. Blackwell

Long before television shows, such as *Fashion Police* (2002), a single name stood out as the barometer of Hollywood *haute couture:* Mr. Blackwell. His annual Worst Dressed List was either eagerly anticipated or loathed, depending on which side of the clothing you were on. The man, who started out life as "Richard Selzer," then as juvenile actor as either "Richard Selzer," "Dick Selzer," or "Richard Blackwell," only to emerge as a fashion designer and later a fashion critic, had a journey fraught with peril and poverty. It was the subject of his book, *From Rags to Bitches*, an autobiography he was promoting in June 1995, when we had a lengthy conversation on the radio.

Right from the start, he shared his early hard knock life, describing what his book was about.

BLACKWELL: Well, there's a story of a man not born with a great silver spoon in his mouth and a crystal chandelier over his head, and someone who didn't drive a Rolls Royce to the nearest bistro gardens. There's a story of survival. There's the story of a man born in Brooklyn, who did not have even a home to sleep in. There's the story about a man who never knew his father. There's the story about a man who had three years of grade school education, and then goes on to Broadway, and then goes on to Hollywood, and all of a sudden, the whole world seems to open up, and there is something wonderful and fantastic to talk about.

You could hear some of the pain in Mr. Blackwell's voice, as he reminisced about some of the darker episodes of his youth. He wrote his book because he felt his story had to get out. He stressed survival was the biggest message he wanted to convey with his story.

BLACKWELL: I remember when I was a much younger man. I remember looking for someone who would listen to me. I remember wanting someone to listen to me. I remember sitting in an alley under a fire escape, crying my eyes out, saying, "Isn't there anyone who would love me?" I remember wanting someone just to hold my hands and say, "I'm so glad you're here." I remember having to pay a price, when I was in the dress business, for an order by having to have a relationship with buyers that would absolutely nauseate me. I remember having wonderful romances in Hollywood with people who would probably say, "Oh really!" But these people held out their hand and they said, "We love you, even for a moment, we love you!" It's a little thing called "have a little faith." It's a little thing about saying, "Okay, it happened. It wasn't bad, it was only an experience." There's something here about a man who says, "I needed love," and took it any place it came. It's a man who did a lot of things other people might have been ashamed of or embarrassed about, but it did not embarrass me. It's the story about a man who lived every alternative lifestyle you can imagine.

Through the course of the conversation, Mr. Blackwell repeated his earlier desires to get attention and be noticed. I questioned whether his success came out of a deeper need just to be loved.

BLACKWELL: I think a lot of my success has been driven by the desire to be accepted. If you've ever been alone, and never knew your father, and never knew where a meal was coming from, all you really wanted was someone to need you for something. And then love became something that was probably the most emotional need you had. And you were absolutely willing to accept it under any condition, under any term.

Mr. Blackwell's story was a cautionary tale, not because he didn't want anyone to repeat his life experiences, but rather because he didn't want people to feel alone or ashamed of where they came from.

BLACKWELL: I don't want those people to say, "Is there something wrong with me?" No, there's nothing wrong with any human being who has any desire, different as it may be, there is nothing wrong with any human being who says, "Alright, I live this way, but I will do it well. I will do it with class and I will do it with dignity."

As a young actor, Blackwell worked with the likes of Mae West and Howard Hughes, the latter he was under contract with. He was in a small, unaccredited role in *Little Tough Guy* (1938), which was as part of another group of juveniles similar to the *Dead End Kids*. He believed those early days of acting took him away from homelessness and saved his life.

BLACKWELL: I honestly believe, Peter—and I mean this will all my heart—that if I had not been discovered, I would have been gone. I don't think you survive in that environment. If you make another day, you're lucky. You know how we used to live under a fire escape, Peter? I'm not asking the question, because you couldn't possibly, possibly in your wildest dreams, imagine this. We would break a milk bottle and hold the neck by the hand. And if anyone came towards us in our sleep, we would reach out and jab. And if we didn't jab, we would probably be killed.

How does someone who literally has to sleep with one eye open to survive get discovered in showbiz? Mr. Blackwell believed a lot of it was luck. He was a rough and tumble homeless youth living in underprivileged neighborhoods. On Broadway, the play, *Dead End* (1935), featured characters living the same experience. He auditioned for a role in a road company version that toured later. He added realism to the acting.

BLACKWELL: When they took a look at me, they said, "He looks the part. People will look at him and understand his emotions." That was the main thing. So, I went into a road company of *Dead End* itself. I played Tommy, the leader. I forgot ninety-five percent of my lines, but as [dramatist] Sidney Kingsley said, "We're not interested in the exact words. What we're trying to show people is there is a society that lives in this manner."

From there, along with his mother, he was off to Hollywood, where not only did the sun shine a little more, but life got a little brighter. His mother managed to get odd jobs, while he got into the door at Universal Studio thanks to the mother of the Andrew Sisters.

PETER: You've gone from literally the streets of Brooklyn, New York, into the world of Broadway and Hollywood, and that is a major monumental leap on its own.

BLACKWELL: But you've got to remember, we got there through an alley.

PETER: Exactly.

BLACKWELL: We did not get there eating at Club 21.

PETER: And then, on top of that, the acting career goes okay to a certain degree, but you decide, for one reason or another, maybe this is not what you should be doing and you go into the world of fashion, which is an entirely different direction, and became successful there. That in itself is another leap, sometimes hard to believe.

BLACKWELL: Well, do you know sometimes people don't let doors open for them? Sometimes, people turn things away. People say, "Well I could have done it if . . . ." or "I could have done it, but . . . ." And that's not the case. There's a lot of things, by the way, that happened in between that. Going in the dress business was the result of doing costumes for a girl I was managing. She was a nightclub singer. Well, the reviews of her clothing were far better than of her voice, so when the girl totally bombed out, I took those reviews downtown to a manufacturer and looked around for somebody who would give me a job. I had no idea. I mean, I wasn't bright or brilliant. I was just following very ordinary common, I suppose, street gut feeling.

PETER: Where did your sense of fashion first come from?

BLACKWELL: Where does a boy at five years old learn to play Chopin? How does that happen? I think maybe God gives us a wonderful gift and the ability to do these things and we don't question them. And the most important thing is we simply go ahead and we do them. The first year I was a designer, I became almost the rage of the fashion industry, because I dared defy everybody else who was doing clothes I thought were not as pretty and did what I believed was beautiful.

PETER: That must have annoyed your contemporaries at the time?

BLACKWELL: Well, they blacklisted me. As a matter of fact the very first ad we ever did—and we did the ad figuring this—I can admit it now. The ads at the time, believe it or not, were $3,000 a page. We were very new in business, so we decided to do an ad in both *Harper's Bazaar* and *Vogue Magazine*. The accountant had told us we were bankrupt unless something major had happened. We just simply didn't have the accounts and we didn't have the money. So, we decided on taking the ad figuring, *Well, what if I can't pay for it? I mean, what are they going to do? They're going to take a cutting table? You know, they can come and take the cutting table.* It wouldn't have made any difference. But I did something so unusual that I became almost the conversation of 7th Avenue.

PETER: Was that when you used the ad of just your own face?

BLACKWELL: The big portrait of me.

While his fashions led to success, his list made him a household name. In 1960, *American Weekly Magazine,* a supplement found in Sunday newspapers, asked him to create a Best Dressed and Worst Dressed list. Half the audience was outraged by it, but the other half loved it. The annual list was slow to grow in popularity.

BLACKWELL: We tried it every year the same time, but it took three full years for it really to take hold. And by the time it took hold, it just exploded wide open. Now, nobody thought of me as a dress designer. Nobody thought of me as a kid who had ever been an actor. Most of them didn't even know it. They thought of the man who does the list. And that's what I was basically known for.

It was the acerbic comments that drew attention. When Geena Davis wore a yellow dress with mesh hosiery and a big tail behind it, he referred to her as "Big Bird in heels; a Follies Bergere fiasco." About Cher, he said, "A million beads and one overexposed derriere." On Martha Stewart, "Dresses like the centerfold for *Farmers' Almanac.*"

The biggest buzz when *From Rags to Riches* came out was talk of Mr. Blackwell's personal relationships.

PETER: One of the things that is very controversial about the book is it talks about some of the people you have had relationships with, and this came as a surprise to quite a few people. I'm wondering if you've heard from any of the families, friends, and relatives of those you have had relationships with that you talk about in the book, and if they have anything negative or positive to say about it.

BLACKWELL: No, and do you know something? I really don't believe I'm going to. They began to lead completely different lives. You know, we're talking about a good many years ago. I was twenty years old, and they were new in the studios. They were not married. It isn't as if they were married and lived a second kind of a life. These people were never married, at that point, and then the studios demanded they get married in order to save their career.

PETER: We should mention for those listening who have no idea what we are talking about, you have had relationships with some prominent male actors.

BLACKWELL: Alright, and we can even tell you who they were. It was Tyrone Power, it was Randy Scott, and I will tell you here and now I am neither ashamed nor embarrassed about it. You see, I had no father. I had nobody who ever gave a darn whether I was standing, sitting, dead, or alive, and when these people offered me any sense of love, any sense of affection, I grabbed it. I was delighted somebody cared I was alive. I didn't look at it as anything I had to be ashamed of. And one of the things this book is going to do is it's going to tell a lot of kids you can live any life you choose, just do it well. It's going to tell a lot of people, it's okay. No one's going to set the rules for you anymore. The rules are "do it well, have respect for who you're with, and love."

After leading a life with such dramatic twists and turns, I was curious to know who could play the charismatic Mr. Blackwell if a movie was made. He said it would take at least three actors to cover the various stages of his long life, but the bulk of the screen time should go to John Malkovich.

BLACKWELL: I think he's an incredible actor. I think he has many faces. I think he can look any way you would choose him to do, and I think he is the ultimate in class.

It's hard to imagine the actor who could bring this larger than life character to the screen, but a film depiction of Mr. Blackwell would earn him the recognition and love he pursued all through his life.

Esther Williams. Photo courtesy of Harlan Boll.

Chapter 28

Esther Williams

She was beautiful, she was talented, and she was athletic, a winning combination leading to a film genre uniquely all her own. Esther Williams was a big star in the heyday of MGM Studios, when her pool-based movies entertained millions.

Williams made a big splash on our show in June 2002. Always the businesswoman, she was embarking on a new venture in the hopes of bringing the spectacle of the water musicals she was known for in the movies to the live stage in Las Vegas. Think Cirque du Soleil underwater. Her new venture was an excuse to go down memory lane to the beginning of her career.

Her life in the pool started at a young age growing up in Los Angeles.

WILLIAMS: The Los Angeles Athletic Club would scout the city playground meets to find prospective swimmers and I was certainly that!

Noting that there were plenty of baseball diamonds but no swimming pools in her neighborhood, Williams' mother, Bula, a take charge kind of woman, got the ball rolling to get a community pool for her then eight-year-old daughter. Bula went to Parks and Recreation and gave them an ultimatum.

WILLIAMS: She said, "You put a swimming pool in that Manchester Playground and [my daughter] will donate her time to inaugurating it for you." And they said, "What does that mean?" She said, "She'll swim across and you give her a little medal and she will think it's the Olympics, she'll be very happy." And so, my mother, who was a wonderful, ahead-of-her-time lady, had done what protesters and lobbyist couldn't do. She said, "You have to treat the women right, and little girls are going to be women someday. So, you make a swimming pool in that playground for her, and she'll pay you back by being a champion."

The pool was built, young Esther swam to inaugurate it, and they gave her a medal, but something else had her hooked.

WILLIAMS: I was probably nine by the time I did that swim across the pool. When I got out of the water and everybody applauded, I said, "Oh, this is fun!" I liked the applause, and I still do!

You could hear the love in Williams' voice, when she talked about her mother and the influence she had on her, but it was her older sister who did much of the raising of Esther.

WILLIAMS: Oh, I just loved Bula Williams. I was her fifth child, and she had been awfully busy raising my four brothers and sisters. By the time she got to the fifth one, she turned to my older sister, Maurine, and said, "You raise this one. I'm going to go and find out what's going on in the world." She was very liberated very early. My sister Maurine taught me to swim. She took me to the beach on the streetcar. We managed. We didn't have a lot of money, but we sure had a lot of "do it!" Like Nike says, "Just do it!"

Williams didn't realize she was a cut above the rest in the pool at an early age, but she did know being in the water was the best she was going to feel all day. It was by chance that she hung out with the lifeguards, swimming as they did laps, matching them stroke for stroke.

WILLIAMS: I had no idea of the benefits I would reap from that. They were the best coaches I ever had, because they were so supple and those lovely long muscles, strong, that they save people with, were the most wonderful teachers in the world. By the time I got into competitive swimming, they said that little girl can swim.

At fifteen years old, she was representing the Los Angeles Athletic Club Swim Team, winning more than her share of races.

WILLIAMS: Because of those lifeguards, I learned to swim butterfly breaststroke long before women, or even men for that matter, were doing it. That's where you throw the arms forward, but instead of in the water, you're out of the water, so it's like a double crawl. It makes you awfully strong to swim that stroke. Strong is what I needed to win races.

PETER: Did you do any other work in the gym to strengthen yourself, or was it just all working in the pool?

WILLIAMS: We had the word of our coaches that they didn't even want us to walk at the beach in the sand, because they were afraid it would tie up our muscles and our legs and the calves. It was all nonsense, of course, because now they use pulleys and do all kinds of things in the gym simulating swimming. But then, they didn't want you to do anything but swim. Just get in the water and go at it, because they thought all the other sports—running, jogging, even walking—they thought you would strain those muscles they believed needed to be supple to swim.

Williams' conversation came back to the overwhelming positive influence of her mother, even when talking about exercise. She immediately went into the story of when she broke a record in the butterfly during a medley relay race. Since records weren't kept for individual accomplishment during a medley relay race, the powers that be wanted Williams to swim alone the following week to see if she could match or beat her record breaking performance, thus making it official—yet again, they didn't want her to do anything but swim during the week.

WILLIAMS: I broke the rule from my coach and went to the beach and rode breakers. There was a very sharp shell in the water in the sand. I stepped on it and cut my foot wide open. What a sight to see the inside of your foot! They called the lifeguards, and they took me home, and when I went into the house on crutches, my Mother said, "Esther, if you didn't want to swim in the meet next Sunday, you didn't have to cut your foot!" That's the kind of mother I had!

Williams made the U.S. Olympic Swim Team and was destined to compete in the XII Olympiad in Helsinki, Finland in 1940. However, World War II dashed her hopes, and the Games were cancelled. Williams didn't brood over the cancellation, in part, because of the eternal optimism of her mother. When Esther told Bula the Games were cancelled, her only response was, "Well, you can't eat medals. What are you gonna do?

Bula Williams correctly surmised that there wouldn't be an Olympics for at least eight years, so her daughter might as well do something else. That something else was to turn professional. Esther swam for Billy Rose's Aquacade.

PETER: Did you ever feel you missed out by not being at the Olympics when you look back at all the things you have done in your career?

WILLIAMS: Well, I heard a story once about Harry Truman. He had a haberdashery shop in Independence, Missouri. He failed. He wasn't a good salesman. Somebody once said to Harry, "Why couldn't you make your haberdashery shop a success?" He said, "Well, it went broke." But he said, "As a consolation prize, they made me President of the United States." And I took that story and said if there can't be an Olympics, I'll become a star and it will be in the movies.

PETER: You go to Billy Rose's Aquacade, and from there, you're discovered by MGM.

WILLIAMS: MGM came up to see me, and I couldn't believe they were going to make a swimming musical. Seemed to me it was a one picture thing that could happen and you'd never do it again, but they had seen the grosses of Sonja Henie and her ice skating pictures, and she was an athlete and a champion. They said, "Let's just melt the ice and toss a swimmer in there and see what happens." I said, "God, they're ready for mackerels to be stars! We'll see what we can do." I just did my best. I was there for eighteen years, and I was in the Top 10 box office for seven years, and I figured that was my Harry Truman consolation prize. It was better than being President of the United States!

PETER: When MGM first came to you, did you have any acting experience, school plays, anything like that?

WILLIAMS: Nothing. I never even got an autograph. When they told me they were going to sign me to a contract, I said, "Well, you people have a lot of courage, because I can't sing and I can't act and I can't dance, but I can sure swim, and if you think you can make a movie out of that, I congratulate you, but if you don't want me, just throw me back in the pool, I'll be okay." That was my Mother's theory about everything, and I guess I picked that up.

PETER: With all the swimming you've done in the movies, take after take after take, it's not easy. How did you deal with things like chlorine in the pool? Was there any concern with what it was doing to your skin, your hair, and considering you had to be in makeup for the movies? Was this a problem?

WILLIAMS: Well, it was no problem. It was before doctors had us so scared about melanoma on our skin. I kept a good tan all year round, because body makeup came off in the water. But what happens with swimming, the longer you're in the water, the more you're swimming, what you can do staying under the water at nine o'clock in the morning, you can do twice as well, three times as well at 4:30 in the afternoon, because you've been in the water all day. And somehow the body, in its miraculous ability to adjust, switches over. I used to check my mirror to see if I grew gills like a fish (laughter)!

Williams was nineteen when she signed with the studio, but like her childhood in the pool, she was a fast learner, quickly picking up the skills she needed to be a star. And perhaps drawing from the same savvy gene pool of her mother, she also knew when to get out of the movie business.

WILLIAMS: I knew when I saw Eleanor Powell's feet bleeding because she danced too much, and when [Joan] Crawford was so broken hearted because nobody wanted her anymore in pictures, I said, "There's an end to this thing, and I think when you have this kind of success you better hedge your bet." And so, I went into business."

In 1958, Williams started her swimming pool company. Not only was she fortunate to have a good business sense, she also had good timing on her side.

WILLIAMS: There was a gas shortage and nobody could get to their favorite watering hole or lake or river or whatever. So, I said, "They've got to have a swimming pool in the backyard. It needs to be affordable and in fast because everybody signs up for a swimming pool and they want it yesterday." So, I had a tremendous success with a thing called The Esther Williams Swimming Pool.

Williams also designed a successful line of swimsuits that, for years, bore her name. She always thought the movie business was a perfect segue for her into business in general.

WILLIAMS: Both of those things deal with the audience. You give them something that makes sense for you to endorse, and it's appropriate, and what they say is, "I've always wanted to look like her in the water. So, I've got to get a suit that will make me look like her." So, I designed them very carefully after things I had worn in the pictures.

PETER: People who listen to this show on a regular basis will know what I'm about to say right now, but this might come as a surprise to you, Esther. I am one of those people terrified of water.

WILLIAMS: Oh, you poor baby!

PETER: I do not swim. I don't even get on boats.

WILLIAMS: You know I solved that. I know about that phobia. I wrote a book, *Swim, Baby Swim*, in which I explained how to make a baby safe in the water. I'm talking at six months and at a year they're swimming. I felt so good about it because I had this grandson just born to my daughter and they lived with me for awhile after [husband] Fernando [Lamas] died in 1982. Suzie was pregnant with little Thomas, and I was there when he was born. I said to Suzie, "We've got to teach this baby how to swim." Because I have a pool that's attached to my house, and it would be an eyesore to put a fence around it, I said, "Let's just fence the kid." And so, I taught him to swim, and he was swimming at a year, easily and certainly safe in the water, because there's a way to teach a baby how to float until Mommy can get off that damn phone and take care of her kid in the water, because that's when they drown. You can't turn your back on a small child in the water.

In talking to Williams, there was never any doubt of her love for the pool and the benefits derived from it. Before going to air, we set up the call for the appropriate time. I knew she had recently suffered a broken ankle, but I was still surprised to be told that she was coming to the phone as quickly as she could because she was just getting out of the pool. Williams was an evangelist for the therapeutic benefits of swimming.

WILLIAMS: I'm bionic. I've had a hip replacement, because all that bouncing on diving boards had taken away all the cartilage in my hip and my leg. And I got back into the water just as soon as the wounds healed and amazed doctors on how quickly I healed. Every doctor, instead of a gym doing physical therapy, should have a pool. So, I'm on my full weight on my ankle and they're amazed at how quickly it's happened, but I'm not, because I know it's the pool.

Even though Williams never made it into an Olympic competition, she did leave a lasting impression on the World Games.

WILLIAMS: We have this wonderful, and you should excuse the expression, pool of synchronized swimmers, and I was very influential in getting that wonderful sport into the Olympics.

Synchronized swimming has been part of the Olympics since the 1984 games, hosted in her home town of Los Angeles. So, Esther's mother—the visionary—was right all along. Convincing the city to build a pool for her talented daughter would reap benefits for years to come.

Lindsay Wagner.

Chapter 29

Lindsay Wagner

Lindsay Wagner literally jumped into our living rooms in the 1970s, not only because of her role as Jamie Sommers, the *Bionic Woman*, but because of the smart, intelligent characters she was determined to play in a business that too often undervalued and trivialized female roles.

We had an extended conversation on the radio in late January 2009. By coincidence, three weeks before she was on the air, I talked to her two grown sons, Dorian and Alex Kingi. Dorian was making a name for himself as a film director, while Alex was carving a green path with his eco-friendly clothing company. I brought that up at the start.

PETER: We're working our way, apparently, through your entire family.

WAGNER: (laugher) I know! I told my mother, "Be expecting a call."

PETER: We had your sons on a few weeks ago talking about the things they're doing—very impressive stuff, by the way.

WAGNER: Yeah, thanks. I heard the interview. I thought it went really well. You make it very easy, I got to tell you.

Wagner's life was far removed from her days when she came into our homes weekly via television. She was then into experiential workshops and retreats, but it was a journey started back when she was twenty.

WAGNER: My boyfriend's parents, at the time, were very into the body-mind-spirit connection. They were kind of early runners in that whole thing, which is on the cover of *Time* magazine today. When I was quite ill, they offered me the opportunity to work with their mentor, and I actually was able to heal my ulcers through visualization, mediation, and diet.

The experience was an eye-opener for Wagner, who had suffered with ulcers from childhood and was slated to go under the knife to improve her health. She figured there was a lot not being told in the mainstream about health issues.

WAGNER: It's been a lifelong study for me. I really wanted to be a psychologist, not an actress, in the beginning, so it's kind of funny. But I was dyslexic and I couldn't get through college. They didn't have the help they have for people today. So, I continued to study myself on my own time.

As she began her acting career, Wagner discovered she had a knack for sharing the same types of things she was interested in by communicating them through story. Her talent and training as an actress was a plus in getting her message across.

WAGNER: I've always had a real sensitivity to people's energy and emotions. It's kind of annoying in a relationship sometimes because I always feel what's going on with the other person. I was kind of born, I think, with an extra dose of that kind of sensitivity and had to learn how to work with it over the years, because it can be difficult if you don't know how to shut it off at times.

Acting for Wagner was a chance to explore where emotions come from, and in turn it fuelled her teachings, leading to her healing work. As the new millennium began, Wagner focussed less on acting and more on helping others. She started doing counselling, including working in jails with domestic violence offenders.

WAGNER: When they were coming out of jail, I co-facilitated a support group for the families when they were coming back together, and so it's kind of something that's evolved, it's grown over the last ten years. It's been about nine years, not that I haven't done a film, but I guess I can say the work I've done, and the study I've done, and the personal work I've done, is to me the very best way you can go about becoming a better actor.

PETER: When you're counselling people in jails in situations like that, isn't it kind of surreal when you walk into jail and somebody says, "Isn't that the Bionic Woman?"

WAGNER: (laugher) It is for a few minutes. Interestingly enough, I wondered how that was going to play out, but I think it actually helps in a lot of ways, because in my career, not just in *The Bionic Woman*, I've done about forty television movies and a handful of features, but the movies I did were very intentionally for television. All those films, most of them, were issue-oriented movies, and I don't necessarily mean political, I mean interpersonal issues. We covered a lot of issues, so I think people in general who followed my career, though they say "Oh, *The Bionic Woman*," they've had an experience over the years of the fact my work relates to interpersonal stuff; it's not just drama or sensational stuff. And so, I think I somehow have developed through that a relationship with the audience to where it didn't seem like such a strange thing to them. It was kind of fun and freaky at first. They'd say, "Oh, my God, I can't believe she's here," and then I start to talk, and we start to share, and then they start to talk to me, and all of a sudden that's gone. We're just two humans sitting there sharing.

Her ease at talking with people was quite evident during our conversation. I was even willing to divulge my early devotion to the craft of Lindsay Wagner. I shared with her my teenage years of working as a theater usher. As a fifteen-year-old, the first film I worked at was *The Paper Chase* (1973), a classic film of hers, and I saw it over and over again for the four months it played. I was also lucky enough to see a little-known Canadian film she starred in called *Second Wind* (1976).

PETER: The thing I would say about both of those roles, and a lot of the roles you played, was that there seems to be a cookie cutter image people have in Hollywood of the young starlet, but you kind of broke that mould, because your characters probably had a higher IQ than most characters other females were having a chance to play at the time. Would you say that's correct? And was that something you strove for, or were you just lucky in that regard?

WAGNER: Oh no, that was very . . . I mean, I didn't think of it in terms of IQ, but for me I was only interested in doing things that for me was a communication, because, in a way, this was almost like my fallback profession. If it didn't have something to say about human beings, if I didn't feel like I could be sharing something with someone that was meaningful to me, most of the time, it didn't really interest me. Once in a while, there was something kind of fun or fluffy and was fun to do, but I get bored with that really quickly. Many of the films I did I actually did a lot of rewriting on, to take a story that was kind of a basic drama and really infuse interpersonal processes in it, wanting to share at least my experience at any given point in my personal evolution; things that have helped me and perspectives I've seen and grown through and come to another way of viewing things. Hopefully, I always wanted to take from the beginning of a story to the end of a story, take somebody through it, not just survive the circumstance but actually transcend whatever state my character was in.

Wagner's most famous role began as a guest shot on a two-part episode of *The Six Million Dollar Man*. ["The Bionic Woman" broadcast on March 16, 1975.] In it, she was the girlfriend of Steve Austin, played by Lee Majors. Wagner wasn't a sci-fi fan and had not seen the show, so reading the concept of the script was somewhat foreign to her. But she talked to her mother on the phone, asking if she had ever seen the show. Her mother let her know that *The Six Million Dollar Man* was the favorite program of Lindsay's then thirteen-year old sister. Plus, the shooting schedule was slated to begin on her sister's birthday. It was a perfect way to end her contract with Universal. The two-part episode led to her character's death and she would be free and clear.

In the script, the death of Jamie Sommers became a reality because the studio didn't want to tie down their hero with a girlfriend, yet after the episode aired, the fans were not happy with Jamie's tragic end.

WAGNER: All the kids were already very attached to that kind of quintessential, idyllic, father figure protector, and they created the female counterpart and then killed her right in front of all these kids' eyes. Well, the public outrage was what actually brought about the next episode. ["The Return of The Bionic Woman," 1975.]

By the time that episode aired and the fan fallout began, Wagner was no longer under contract with Universal and was in Canada shooting *Second Wind*, but the pressure was mounting.

WAGNER: They aired the episode, everybody was going crazy, and I started getting calls saying would you please come back and do another episode? We have to bring you back to life.

The resurrection of Jamie Sommers was complete and the popularity of the character was not lost on the suits at *ABC*. They saw the potential for a spinoff series.

WAGNER: The kids were flat out traumatized. One of the letters they actually convinced me to come back with was from someone at Boston Children's Hospital. Someone there was ripping into the network for irresponsible programming saying, "You don't think about the affect you have on children when you do these stories?" So, I said, "Ow-ee, we gotta do this."

The Bionic Woman was born. ["Welcome Home, Jamie, a two-part episode broadcast on January 14 and 21, 1976.] The opportunity to be a role model for children and be able to teach them was not lost on Wagner, who used to teach acting to kids as therapy. It was the best of both worlds, as her agreement with the studio allowed her input in making the scripts more meaningful. She shared a wide variety of articles with the writers about such topics as mind over matter and Eastern philosophies, giving the show a deeper purpose than the usual good guy vs. bad guy morality play of the week.

WAGNER: I was constantly pushing them to go deeper with our various stories and to write about our so-called adversaries in not such a black and white way. Whenever possible, I was kind of nudging them to show that people do what they do whether you think it's right or wrong, not because they want to be bad or wrong, and it's our perspective that even tells us it's bad or wrong.

PETER: Does it surprise you that there are such heartfelt thoughts about the show that has been off the air for so many years? People still talk about your role as *The Bionic Woman*. You are still attached to that character.

WAGNER: When you think about it, not just as a TV show, and all of that . . . to me, I tried to make the show and the character more like a mentor instead of just a superhero. We worked very hard. In a series, I'm sure you know, it's so fast and furious how you have to work. To have the time to infuse a lot of meaning is tough. But boy, we gave it our best, and I think that effort was felt by the audience. And at that age to see compassion . . . because again, what do we do when we watch? We identify with somebody, right?

PETER: Yes.

WAGNER: We identify with some character or another when we're watching any kind of a film. So, to even have the one you know is going to win in the story be able to see the person we're going out after, because we feel that's the best thing we should do, as a human being with their own agendas and their own feelings and beliefs and have compassion for that person, even though you have to do something about it. I can't believe that isn't a lifelong impact, because I just know the people in my youth . . . things I remember that stood out to me, were things that made me feel hopeful no matter whether I was doing something bad or something good.

Wagner derives a lot of pride for being a role model for young girls. At a time when there weren't dramatic shows fronted by women, her series led the charge.

WAGNER: It was ground breaking in that sense, and when they found it was well received by the audience, there were a whole slew of them that came very quickly thereafter.

Wagner was disappointed, however, by the shows that followed. She felt subsequent series used the opportunity of a female lead, but the writers lacked a woman's touch and perspective in scripting the shows.

WAGNER: It's almost like they were writing shows they've always written, with men resolving problems. In that concept, we were trying to go beyond, and have more of a feminine slant to problem solving.

Wagner pointed out that on the show she seldom did an offensive move on an adversary. It's something she stressed, daring us all to go back and look at the episodes to prove her point.

WAGNER: Knocking down a tree to impede their way as opposed to coming up and bashing somebody and saying, "I win because I'm stronger." Trying to use the mind so you don't have to hurt someone or setting a trap, that takes a lot more effort on the writers' part.

PETER: During that time period, or even after, could you ever possibly go jogging without someone humming that music behind you?

WAGNER: Oh, my gosh, I couldn't go jogging at all! People would keep stopping me and asking me for an autograph (laughter). Yeah, it was pretty intense there for a while. It was kind of freaky when you first, all of a sudden, lose your anonymity and you can't go anywhere. I mean people say, "Oh that would be so much fun!" Okay, you try it! (Laughter.) It's really odd. Your psyche has a real serious adjustment to go through.

Wagner's experience in playing Jamie Sommers gave her a respect for science fiction.

WAGNER: I realized it was a genre you could do and say all the kinds of things you want to say, but if you said them in normal circumstances, often times people would say, "That's crazy, people would never do that." But in sci-fi you can just say it.

She could have been another iconic character, but the role slipped through her fingers even before she knew she had a chance for it. After actress Geneviève Bujold dropped out of the lead in Star Trek: Voyager (1995-2001), and before Kate Mulgrew got the part, there was talk of Wagner being looked at to play Captain Kathryn Janeway.

WAGNER: Honestly, I didn't even know about it. I didn't get the offer. What we figured happened afterwards was my agent had gotten the inquiry, but at one point earlier I had said I wasn't into doing a series again at the time. And there were very few things I could have imagined I wanted to do, and sadly, that was one of them! So, at the time, she [her agent] just said, "She doesn't want to do a series," so it was turned down and I never even knew the offer was there.

Wagner wasn't against the idea of returning to television, however the role had to be right. Her life was full with all the work and teaching she'd been doing since she stepped away from in front of the camera. There was never a dull moment for her, and I can't imagine anyone having a dull conversation with her. Talking about her teachings and her workshops, I got the feeling that Lindsay Wagner was exactly where she needed to be, and the people she came in contact with were better for it.

Tippi Hedren. Photo courtesy of Bill Dow.

Chapter 30

Tippi Hedren

Much had been said and written about the type of women film director Alfred Hitchcock was attracted to—a type played by Janet Leigh, Kim Novak, Grace Kelly, and Tippi Hedren—women who could be equal parts terrified victims and conniving vixens.

To be a Hitchcock heroine was to exist in a master class of acting, and in many cases to being controlled. Revelations about the dark side of the macabre genre director later came to light, but that wasn't always the case. I've spoken to Tippi Hedren on several occasions over the years, starting with a conversation in September 2002, back then she touted the praises of working with "Hitch."

PETER: Is it a happy set working on a Hitchcock film? You appeared in two of them.

HEDREN: Most of the time, it was really quite incredibly wonderful, because it was working with Hitchcock, who, of course, is a genius and the best at building suspense. And just watching the way he worked was a thrill. I don't know if he directed me differently, because *The Birds* (1963) was my first movie. [Tippi had appeared in an earlier, unaccredited role in Columbia Pictures' *The Pretty Girl* (1950).] So, he was not only my director, he was my drama coach, which was fabulous.

PETER: Alfred Hitchcock was notorious, at least in quotes, for saying some rather nasty things about actors.

HEDREN: Oh, are you talking about "Actors should be treated as cattle," or "They are cattle?"

PETER: But there is not a bad quote—in fact, there are great quotes—about you, Tippi Hedren, from Hitchcock.

HEDREN: Oh, well that's really lucky.

PETER: He seems to have really liked you as an actress.

HEDREN: Well, I am very grateful for that, but as far as him saying actors should be treated as cattle, or whatever, most of his best friends were actors. You know, Jimmy Stewart and Carey Grant and Ingrid Bergman, Grace Kelly, so many of them.

Even though *The Birds* was her first major role in a movie and she was working with a legendary filmmaker, Hedren didn't feel intimidated on the set, but recognized the responsibility placed on her as the leading lady.

HEDREN: Hitch gave me the security that I would be able to do this. If he hadn't done that, I don't think I ever could have done it, because it was a tremendous role to take on as a first performance.

Hedren also credits her seasoned co-stars with helping her initially. In *The Birds*, she starred opposite Rod Taylor, Suzanne Pleshette, and stage legend, Jessica Tandy, but most of the praise was left for her director.

HEDREN: I learned so much from Hitch about making a motion picture. He had me sit in on meetings with every department, every phase of making a motion picture. He was very much involved in every phase.

Hitchcock was not known for doing a lot of takes, which Hedren says spoiled her for directors.

HEDREN: I think if I was ever working with a director who was doing ten, twelve, or twenty takes, I'd just say, "Please excuse me. When you figure out what you want, call me back." Hitch was wonderful. Very often it would be the first take he would print, and very often he would say, "Let's just do one more for insurance."

Hedren also recalled a humorous story about the search for her leading man in the second Hitchcock film she appeared in, *Marnie* (1964). Hitchcock had scoured all the current films looking at every hot actor for the role of Mark Rutland. After an exhaustive search, he shared the news of his chosen star, Sean Connery.

HEDREN: "You mean Sean Connery, who just got out of *Dr. No*? The Sean Connery, who is probably the most handsome man on this planet? The Sean Connery who could melt the iciest of blondes?" I said, "Mr. Hitchcock, do you remember the character of Marnie is so frigid she screams every time a man comes near her? How am I supposed to handle that?" And he paused, and looked down his nose at me, and said, "It's called acting, my dear!" That was just his wry sense of humor.

However, when I caught up with Hedren for what would be our fourth conversation in 2012, the story was slightly different. It was a time when Hitchcock was the subject of both a theatrical release and an *HBO* film. The *HBO* entry was called *The Girl* [a 2012 British television film directed by Julian Jarrold and produced by the BBC and HBO Films.] The title refers to a nickname Hitchcock allegedly had for Hedren, and it tells the story of Hedren's experience with Hitchcock and how he was overly possessive, controlling, and very demanding. After she rebuffed his advances on her, he proceeded to make life difficult for her on the set.

PETER: Tippi, I wanted to ask you about working with Hitchcock, because now the stories are coming out about the problems you had with Hitch, but we really didn't hear a lot about this back in the day, did we?

HEDREN: No, we didn't, because it was in the studio era. There was nothing I could do. No matter who I talked to, they said there was nothing they could do. I wasn't the only one this happened to. Two of the Hitchcock women became pregnant to get out of their contract.

PETER: I happened to see *The Girl* just the other day. Have you seen the finished product?

HEDREN: Yes, I have. I've seen it twice.

PETER: Was it difficult at all for you to watch it?

HEDREN: Yes, it was very difficult for me to watch, and I don't know when I'll want to see it again, because it is a rather unhappy, drastic time in my life. You know, the thing I keep thinking, and I mentioned this to Hitchcock at one point, I said, "Why are you doing this? Why are you ruining this incredible working relationship we had?" Because I really loved working with him. He was brilliant. He was brilliant as my director. He was brilliant as my drama coach. To have this horrible burden put upon me was unbearable.

PETER: As the *HBO* movie depicts, his wife, Alma, knew what was going on. Was she really complicit in all of this?

HEDREN: Well, apparently she was. I think their relationship was an enigma to all of Hollywood. I don't think anybody understood it. I certainly didn't. Nobody did. At one point, she said to me, "I'm so sorry you have to go through this." And I just looked at her and said, "But Alma, you could stop it!" And her eyes sort of glazed over, and she turned and walked away.

Hedren had input in the making of *The Girl*.

HEDREN: I worked with the producers and the writer, so it is very factual. The writer, Gwyneth Hughes, came out to the reserve and we talked for several hours about the film and the importance of it. Then, when she went back to England to write, she contacted me often about the screenplay.

One scene in *The Girl* revisits the set of *The Birds*, depicting a pivotal moment when Hedren's character, Melanie Daniels, ventures into the attic where she is attacked. Hedren said that Hitchcock lied about the scene. It was her understanding that mechanical birds would be used, but it was always his intention to have real ones.

HEDREN: There wasn't a mechanical bird in sight. However, there were four crates of ravens and gulls and a few pigeons thrown in. There were four bird trainers, who had gauntlets up to their shoulders and they hurled birds at me for a week. So, it was a week of a nightmare. By Friday, they had me on the floor, and they tied the birds to me. One of them jumped from my shoulder and so narrowly missed my eye that I just got all the birds off me and I sat in the middle of the set and just burst into tears of sheer exhaustion.

After starring in Hitchcock's *Marnie*, Hedren severed all ties with the director. She couldn't reconcile the way he personally treated her, but that never took away from what she saw as the genius of his artistry. That's why, despite all the turmoil, she still spoke glowingly when Hitchcock was honoured with an American Film Institute Award in 1979 and went to his funeral in 1980.

HEDREN: I've been able to totally separate the fact he was an absolutely brilliant entity in the film industry, absolutely brilliant! And he will always and should be always remembered as being such. So, I have been able to separate the genius and, unfortunately, the dark side of the man who created the genius.

PETER: Your daughter, Melanie Griffith, is a fine actress in her own right.

HEDREN: Indeed!

PETER: What was it like for you—with all you went through in your career and all the problems and trials and tribulations you had—what was it like for you when your daughter said, "You know, Ma, I think I want to do what you do?"

HEDREN: Well, my daughter didn't know what I went through, because she was so little, and I never talked about it for twenty years, because I was afraid if I talked about it that it would get out in the press and it would be taken the wrong way. So, Melanie didn't know about this whole situation. She was a little girl when I went through all of this with the Hitchcock years. I never told my parents about it. They would have been heartbroken to think I had to go through all of this. So, by the time she decided to go into film, I was surprised because all she knew was it was horrible hours and, you know, it's not all red carpets and klieg lights and excitement and glamour. It's hard work, terrible hours, responsibility of being the lead in a motion picture, and it's an enormous, enormous responsibility. When she decided to do it, you don't realize whether somebody is going to be a success or not until they've done several things. With my daughter, it turned out to be a really fabulous career for her.

Hedren started her rise to fame as a model. She had been very successful in New York, where she modelled and starred in a series of commercials. It was one of those commercials, airing on *The Today Show* that caught the eye of Hitchcock and his wife.

PETER: You were a model at the time. Was it your goal to be an actress?

HEDREN: Not really. In fact, I was at a stage in my modelling career where I was wondering what I was going to do. I had just moved from New York to Los Angeles with my daughter so that Melanie, at three years old, could have some sort of independence, you know, just like saying, "I'm going out to play, Mommy." You certainly can't do that in the streets of New York. So, I had just moved out, and my modelling career did not resume as I expected it to, and I was thinking, *Oh wow, what am I going to do now?* So, I was handed this silver platter [*The Birds*] through the grace of God, actually. So, I worked very hard to be good and to be successful.

Before modelling success in New York, Hedren, who, as a school girl, still had visions of being an ice skating star, experienced the classic Hollywood story of discovery—in her hometown of Minneapolis.

HEDREN: I got off the streetcar coming home from school. A woman handed me her card and said, "Would you have your mother bring you down to Donaldson's Department Store? I'd like to have you model in our fashion shows on Saturday mornings." And that's what started the whole career. I mean everything!"

PETER: You appeared in your first two films with legendary director Alfred Hitchcock, and then you appeared in your third film, *A Countess from Hong Kong* (1967), directed by Charlie Chaplin.

HEDREN: Yes, it was Charlie's last film. It was with Marlon Brando and Sophia Loren. That was amazing, too. It was really all Charlie's directing, because the way he directed was quite unique. He would act out all the parts of the actors in the scene. He'd become Sophia Loren, he'd become me, he'd become Marlon Brando. Well, that didn't go over too well with Marlon Brando.

PETER: Why not?

HEDREN: Well, having someone show him what to do! Oh, my God, no! It didn't work well at all!

PETER: Marlon's more of a method actor.

HEDREN: Oh, you bet he is! The best! Absolutely the best! So, there was a little friction on the set now and then. Other than that, it was incredibly wonderful watching Charlie Chaplin work.

While most fans know her for *The Birds*, a creature of a different kind brought the most fulfilment in Hedren's life. For over forty years, she has been a protector and advocate for big cats. In 1972, she founded Shambala Preserve in California, a refuge for lions, tigers, and other felines, born in captivity and no longer wanted, either by their private owners or zoos and circuses. It was a desire to protect the animals borne out of making the movie *Roar* (1981) in Africa.

PETER: How did your love affair with the animal begin?

HEDREN: Born with it. I like to call it a "birth affect." Some of us are born with it; some of us acquire it later in life, but it always enhances your life so much.

PETER: Not a lot of people have an opportunity to do so much in such a positive way as you have.

HEDREN: Well, everybody can do something positive with anything they find an interest in. Everybody can do that. I must say, I'm way off the board on it. It is my passion to find a home for these animals. These animals were all born in the United States. They were originally all born to be sold as pets.

In addition to the preserve, Hedren has worked with lawmakers to ensure captive felines are properly protected and cared for.

HEDREN: I was successful in getting a federal bill passed. That was just to stop the interstate traffic. It was called The Captive Wildlife Safety Act. I brought it to my own Congressman, Buck McKeon, and he introduced it, and I testified for it.

The bill was passed unanimously in the House and Senate and was signed into law by President George W. Bush in 2003. Meanwhile, Hedren continued to work tirelessly on behalf of the animals, spearheading another legislative drive to stop the breeding of big cats in captivity.

Tippi Hedren was an extremely strong-willed individual, a person who stood up for what she believed with dogged determination. It was the way she's handled her life, her personal career, and her activism, a point brought up in this exchange at the end of our 2012 conversation.

PETER: You certainly kept your daughter sheltered from the situations you dealt with early in your career, and I got to say, to your credit, when people see you on the screen, you made it look easy. No one knew what was going on, at least the fans didn't.

HEDREN: Well, you know, the only thing that was important to me when I was going through all that with Hitchcock was my job. The responsibility of carrying two motion pictures in the female leading role was so huge, and that had more of my attention than anything—and I was going to make those roles as good as I possibly could!

When she uttered that last statement, I could hear the resolve in her voice. Her tone indicated determination and pride, the same tone she used when talking about protecting exotic cats, which was ironic, because a conversation with Tippi Hedren left me with the impression that, in another life, she was one tough mother lion.

Efrem Zimbalist Jr. Photo courtesy of Stephanie Zimbalist.

Chapter 31

Efrem Zimbalist Jr.

From the late 1950s until into the 1970s, Efrem Zimbalist Jr. came into American living rooms weekly playing stoic, no-nonsense heroes, first as Stuart Bailey in ABC's *77 Sunset Strip* (1958-1964), then more famously as Inspector Lewis Erskine on ABC's *The F.B.I.* (1965-1974). It was refreshing to find out the man behind the portrayals was a fun-loving, engaging storyteller, who, unlike his characters, was the life of the party. In late July 2003, Zimbalist made it on to the airwaves with me for an hour-long conversation. He was promoting his autobiography, *My Dinner of Herbs.*

ZIMBALIST: It's a book I wrote with the hope it would bring pleasure to people and not anxiety and unpleasantness and stress or gossip or whatever, but just a book that would help people enjoy an evening or a day or two of reading it.

The fledging days of ABC were filled with Warner Bros. shows, featuring stars under contract to the studio. That left everybody's fate in the shadow cast by the sudden whims of tyrannical studio head Jack Warner, yet Zimbalist managed to survive. He was the star of the long-running *77 Sunset Strip* when Warner struck.

ZIMBALIST: Jack Warner had a fit of temper and fired the whole studio practically. He fired the whole television department, fired all the actors under contract, or let the contracts lapse, and I was the only actor left under contract. There had been about fifty-odd, and he changed at that point the format of *77 Sunset Strip*, which had been on for four years, and just changed it completely, and brought in Jack Webb as a Producer of Television and Bill Conrad as our producer, and we started out on a whole new tact, a totally different show from the old one. Not a bad show, but not at all the show that had been on before and people had come to enjoy. So, it was kind of a terrible shock to the audience. It was a miscalculation in the first order.

The dramatic shift in the show, including a complete cast change, left Zimbalist as the only survivor with a character that resembled Jack Webb's own famous Joe Friday from *Dragnet* (1951). Zimbalist confessed that his portrayal was a bad imitation of Webb, and he wasn't happy with the role, but he was stuck.

ZIMBALIST: There was nothing I could do. I was under contract, and when you were under contract to the studios in those days, if you wanted to get out, you went to court. You sued them and hoped you'd win and so forth, which I never had any desire to do. You just had to do what they told you to do. So, I just did the show. I figured, *They must know something*, so I went ahead, but it only lasted one year.

Zimbalist then spent about a year and a half languishing at Warner Bros. before his next big hit would come along.

ZIMBALIST: After *77 Sunset Strip*, I was really tired of doing a series and I was glad to be out, but in that year and a half, I wasn't very happy with the properties coming my way. I did a couple of good movies and some good television specials, but on the whole I felt it wasn't a very promising period. So, I called my agent and said, "You know, if you could get me a good series,

I'd like to go back into it." And he said, "Well, Warner Bros. has got this series called *The F.B.I.* They've called Quinn Martin to produce it. Let me call them." Well, an hour later, we had a deal, and that's how it all happened.

Coming back from commercial break on the radio, I played the theme song to *The F.B.I.,* which led to this exchange.

PETER: I'm sure, Efrem, that music seems very familiar to you.

ZIMBALIST: You know, I hadn't heard that in such a long time.

PETER: The theme song to the television series, *The F.B.I.* Now I remember when I was a kid watching the show, I always looked forward to the beginning of the brand new season, because I was a big fan of television and I always wanted to know what kind of little changes television shows did to their openings when a new season started. With *The F.B.I.,* the thing I wanted to know is if you would be coming out of that big building and getting into a brand new Ford.

ZIMBALIST: You know, we used to go back to Washington every May. I went back with a skeleton crew and we'd shoot just drive ins and drive outs all around Washington in the new Ford, which wouldn't be out until October. So, they put together a thing which they shipped down to Washington, just for this purpose, and they kept it under wraps in a huge truck, until the moment when I had to get in and drive. And when I got in, it was a total wreck. I mean, there was nothing inside. There was no dashboard; there was no upholstery; there was nothing. It was just a shell, but on the outside it looked like the model that would be out in October. And if you slammed the door it would fall off, I mean, it was stuck together with spirit gum and Scotch Tape. So, I'd drive it around Washington and so forth, and then, after two or three days, they'd put it back in the truck and ship it to Dearborn, where it would be cubed and destroyed, and that would be the end of its life.

PETER: So, the only person who got to drive this car basically was you?

ZIMBALIST: And that was the only thing that was new every year. It was the car and the clothes.

To earn the role of the dapper FBI agent, Zimbalist not only had to get approval from the show's producers, but an affirmative nod from the head of the FBI himself, J. Edgar Hoover.

ZIMBALIST: To Hoover, it sort of represented a training film for the FBI. He felt the FBI was on display. He had turned down 600 applications for series, and then he allowed Warner Bros. to make a movie Mervyn Leroy directed with Jimmy Stewart called *The FBI Story* (1959). He liked it so much they won him over and he agreed to let them to do a series.

Zimbalist became friends with America's top cop, visiting him in Washington every year when the show's crew would shoot exteriors in the capital city.

ZIMBALIST: I knew him quite well, and he wrote to me many, many letters. I have maybe fifty, a hundred letters he wrote me, brief but friendly. He liked the show. He liked what it was doing for the FBI, so we had a very, very good relationship.

The character of Inspector Lewis Erskine was of a man who almost never cracked a smile. He was very straight-laced. That was a challenge for Zimbalist.

ZIMBALIST: If I had been a producer and someone had come to me and said, "I have a great idea for a series. The only thing is the leading character can't smoke, they can't put their hands in their pockets, they can't have anything to do with women, they can't drink, they have to be polite," I'd say, "Great idea. Take it to somebody down the hall, will you?" I mean, it had all the ingredients to make it a stiff bore! And the challenge for me was to have it not be that.

Being a television star wasn't originally in the game plan for Zimbalist. He came to Hollywood to be in movies, but Warner Bros. insisted he shoot a pilot for *77 Sunset Strip*.

ZIMBALIST: They showed me a clause in my contract that said I had to do it if they wanted me to. So, I made the pilot, and it didn't sell; it was turned down by ABC. I was delighted, but they said, "We're going to make another one." So, they made another one, and that one did sell, and that's how *77 Sunset Strip* began. I had just finished a movie I absolutely loved, with a director I loved and a cast, and the thought of going into a TV series at that point was just something I didn't want to do, but as life turned out, TV was very good to me. The fact that most of my life was spent on the small screen is fine with me.

While later actors enjoyed the freedom that came with the end of the old studio system where everybody was locked into a contract without much say in projects, Zimbalist had fond memories of being under contract with Warner Bros.

ZIMBALIST: Oh, I loved it. I thought it was the greatest thing for actors there could be. We weren't paid very much, but we were used. The studio used you in all kinds of things. A lot of things you hated and a lot of things you loved, but they kept you busy. You worked and worked and worked, and that's really what's wonderful. And there was like a protection of your life. They publicized you and they were in back of you, their publicity campaigns and so forth, and they'd build up stars. I think it was a marvelous system.

Zimbalist was born into a highly successful musical family. His father was renowned concert violinist, composer, teacher, and conductor, Efrem Zimbalist Sr., and his mother was operatic soprano Alma Gluck. His parents believed that music was part of an education, so both young Efrem and his sister learned to play instruments. Zimbalist, however, wasn't planning to go into the family business.

ZIMBALIST: I studied the violin for about eight years and developed a modest proficiency in it, but I never wanted to be a violinist, and they never wanted me to be a violinist. It was just the enrichment of life to know an instrument. That was the way they looked at it.

Zimbalist remembered that there were mixed reactions from his parents about his decision to go into showbiz, and he admits that he wanted to be an actor for all the wrong reasons.

ZIMBALIST: I thought it was easy, I thought it was glamorous, there were a lot of beautiful women and a lot of money—all the wrong reasons on Earth, and my mother knew it and she was disgusted with this little flirtation of being an actor. My Father wasn't too happy about it, but he backed me all through my life in anything I wanted to do. He was behind me a hundred percent and he was in this.

PETER: After having experienced the feelings of your parents on your career choice, how did you feel when your own daughter, Stephanie Zimbalist, best-known for her starring role on TV's *Remington Steele* (1982), decided to become an actor?

ZIMBALIST: I said, "There's one thing you have to learn and that is rejection. If you can put up with that, if you can stand it, because you're going to live a life of rejection, people are going to reject you until the day you die. There is no star in Hollywood who hasn't faced that. And if you're willing to do that, then go ahead."

With all he had done in Hollywood, he was most proud of his daughter's success, and nothing gave him more joy than acting with her.

ZIMBALIST: Oh, I was enormously proud, and *appearing* on her show was the greatest thrill I had in Hollywood! I never had anything give me as much pleasure as playing on *Remington Steele*.

Early in his career, Zimbalist played many roles on Broadway, but unlike so many actors who profess to prefer the stage, the repetition of it wasn't his cup of tea.

ZIMBALIST: I love the theater. I love the immediacy of it and the contact with an audience, but I always felt after a certain number of performances—let's say it's three months—there's nothing new that can happen. You're saying the same lines over and over again every night. You've played to every kind of audience there is, the ones who laugh, the ones who snicker, the ones who cry, the ones who applaud. You know them all. There comes a point, I found myself saying, I am bored with doing this every night! The same old thing! All through rehearsal, it's thrilling. You're developing a part, the play is developing, there's excitement of opening night, then there's opening night itself. There's the reviews and the euphoria that lingers after them and so forth, and the first audiences. But, in my opinion, there comes a time when it just becomes redundant. That's what I like about film work, whether it's television or movies. You finish a piece and it's done. Then, you go on to something else. Even if it's a series, it's a different story. I love the theater, but if I had to do something like *Life with Father* for seven years, I'd be in the loony bin.

PETER: You mentioned the reviews. Are you affected by what critics say of your work?

ZIMBALIST: I think you can't help but be a little affected (laughter). It hurts a little if they don't like you. I remember in my early days on Broadway, I appeared in a play of Ibsen's [*Hedda Gabler*, 1948] with Eva Le Gallienne, with my wife [Emily McNair], who is a beautiful actress. Somewhere on the pre-opening tour, we got a review saying the parts of Thea and Eilert Lovborg should be recast. That was hers [Emily's] and my part. It was funny, but it hurt, too. I don't know if you ever . . . Stephanie won't read reviews. She just won't do it. She doesn't want to know if there are bad things said about her. It's a tough situation. There are kind reviewers, people who try to be constructive in their reviews, but there are others who enjoy destroying people, and that hurts.

Besides his own body of work and that of his daughter's, he's most pleased by the reaction of his fans over the years.

ZIMBALIST: I'm so grateful to them for their kindness and support and their interest. It's what you hope, whether it's a series, or a movie, or whatever it is, that it's giving people something that may enrich their lives a little bit. And when you learn it has, it's very, very gratifying. I feel that's the most gratifying thing about my work.

He thought if someone who was having a rough day could sit down, relax, and spend an hour watching his work, and then feel a little better about himself, that was the ultimate of what his profession could do.

ZIMBALIST: I like when it happens. My fans meant the world to me. I enjoyed hearing from them, and I enjoyed writing to them.

After spending an hour Efrem Zimbalist Jr., I felt better about myself, learning that he was an engaging personality and a lot more than just a stoic G-man in a tailored suit.

Epilogue

As I alluded to in the Introduction, conducting an interview was like inviting someone into your home for dinner. I wanted to be civil and make them feel welcome, and I really couldn't let my personal feelings override the conversation at hand. The same rang true even in press conference situations, where I was not the only one asking questions (okay, every once in a while, I wished in a press conference that someone would ask the rude question, but I just hoped it wasn't me.)

I learned this early in my career when I was also working as a film reviewer. Like my faux pas with Christopher Reeve, the comeuppance was again during the 1987 Montreal World Film Festival. Clearly, that year was a sharp learning curve. The teacher in this case was legendary film director Robert Altman.

In the interest of full disclosure, I have to confess that, unlike much of the film-watching world, I was not the biggest Robert Altman fan. While I recognized his mastery as a director, some of his work considered to be the cinematic world's finest, fell flat on me. *Nashville* (1975) didn't appeal, and while I liked *M*A*S*H* (1970), it didn't exactly light my world on fire. I actually enjoyed some of his later work more, such as *Prêt-à-Porter* (1994), and especially *Gosford Park* (2001).

That being said, in 1987, Altman was at the festival to debut his film, *Basements* (1987). Originally shot as a television special for ABC, it featured two one-act plays by Harold Pinter. "The Dumb Waiter" starring John Travolta and Tom Conti, and "The Room" starring Linda Hunt, Julian Sands, and Annie Lennox.

After torturously sitting through the first short film and about a quarter of the second one (thereby breaking my own cardinal rule of watching a film through its entirety before passing judgement), I stormed out of the darkened theater into the bright sunshine loaded for bear. It was only minutes away from a press conference with the auteur and I was determined to be there to get justice for the time I just wasted.

In a conference room packed with press Altman sleepily replied to queries about his film and his craft, politely taking questions from those gathered. When it came to my turn, I angrily bellowed, "Mr. Altman, after just seeing *Basements,* I have to ask—do you ever think of the audience when you're making a film?"

This seemed to wake him up. After a brief moment involving a blank stare, Altman simply replied, "No! I make movies that are my vision, and while I hope they find an audience, that's not my goal. It's to make my art."

Altman, of course, was absolutely correct. What I learned that day was, while the old axiom was that "there are no dumb questions, just dumb answers," there was something to be said about the tone of a question. Despite Altman's thoughtful answer, my question was asked in the wrong context and at the wrong volume. Lesser subjects could have and would have shot the query down with an insult or silence, and they would have been justified. I still had the right to ask such a question, just not in the manner I did. I let my emotions get in the way of the job. I was simply lucky enough to get a worthy sound bite out of it. My combative chat with Robert Altman was the early career course correction I needed to set the foundation for a lifetime of conversations to follow in the future. So, I have to be grateful to Mr. Altman for teaching me a valuable lesson, even though I'll never get back the ninety minutes I spent watching *Basements.*